Anonymous

The Taxation of Property of Railroad Companies in California

As Affected by the Fourteenth Amendment of the Federal Constitution

Anonymous

The Taxation of Property of Railroad Companies in California
As Affected by the Fourteenth Amendment of the Federal Constitution

ISBN/EAN: 9783337414733

Printed in Europe, USA, Canada, Australia, Japan

Cover: Foto ©Suzi / pixelio.de

More available books at **www.hansebooks.com**

THE TAXATION

OF

PROPERTY OF RAILROAD COMPANIES IN CALIFORNIA

AS AFFECTED BY THE

Fourteenth Amendment of the Federal Constitution.

————•————

OPINIONS

OF

JUSTICE FIELD AND JUDGE SAWYER,

DELIVERED IN THE

U. S. CIRCUIT COURT AT SAN FRANCISCO,

SEPTEMBER 17TH, 1883.

——

IN THE

Circuit Court of the United States,

NINTH CIRCUIT,

DISTRICT OF CALIFORNIA.

COUNTY OF SANTA CLARA
vs.
SOUTHERN PACIFIC RAILROAD COMPANY.

COUNTY OF SACRAMENTO
vs.
CENTRAL PACIFIC RAILROAD COMPANY,

And other similar Tax Cases.

SYLLABUS.

1. The property and franchises of the Southern Pacific Railroad Company and of the Central Pacific Railroad Company, corporations created under the laws of California, though the companies are employed by the General Government for postal and military purposes, and were aided by land grants and loans in the construction of their roads, are not exempt from State taxation in the absence of Congressional legislation declaring such exemption. It is competent for Congress to exempt any agencies it may employ for services to the General Government from such taxation as will, in its judgment, impede or prevent their performance.

2. The Fourteenth Amendment of the Constitution, in declaring that no State shall deny to any person within its jurisdiction the "equal protection of the laws," imposes a limitation upon the exercise of all the powers of the State which can touch the individual or his property, including that of taxation.

3. The "equal protection of the laws" to any one implies not only that the means for the security of his private rights shall be accessible to him on the same terms with others, but also that he shall be exempt from any greater burdens or charges than such as are equally imposed upon all others under like circumstances. This equal protection forbids unequal exactions of any kind, and among them that of unequal taxation.

4. Uniformity in taxation requires uniformity in the mode of assessment, as well as in the rate of percentage charged.

5. The thirteenth article of the Constitution of California declares that "a mortgage, deed of trust, contract, or other obligation by which a debt is secured shall, for the purposes of assessment and taxation, be deemed and treated as an interest in the property affected thereby," and that, "except as to railroad and other *quasi* public corporations," the value of the property affected, less the value of the security, shall be assessed and taxed to its owner, and that the value of the security shall be assessed and taxed to its holder, and that the taxes so levied shall be a lien upon the property and security, and may be paid by either party to the security; that if paid by the owner of the security, the tax levied upon the property affected thereby shall become a part of the debt secured ; and if. the owner of the property shall pay the tax levied on the security, it shall constitute a payment thereon, and to the extent of such payment a full discharge thereof. In the assessment of property of the defendants—railroad companies—the mortgages thereon were not deducted, but the whole value of the property, notwithstanding the mortgages thereon, was assessed and the property taxed according to such assessment, to those companies; *Held* (1), treating the mortgages as transferring a taxable interest in the property, that in assessing against the company the interests with which they had at the time parted by their mortgages, and taxing them upon that assessment, was a proceeding to take the property of the companies without due process of law; and (2) treating the mortgages as a lien or incumbrance upon the property, that by not deducting their amount in the assessment of the value of the property of the railroad companies for taxation, as is done in the valuation of property of natural persons, when subject to a mortgage, there was a discrimination against the companies, which resulted in imposing a greater burden upon their property than is imposed upon the property of natural persons.

6. Persons do not lose their right to equal protection guaranteed by the Fourteenth Amendment to the Federal Constitution when they form themselves into a corporation under the laws of California.

7. The State possesses no power to withdraw corporations from the guaranties of the Federal Constitution. Whatever property a corporation lawfully acquires is held under the same guaranties which protect the property of natural persons from spoliation.

8. Under the reserved power to amend, alter, or repeal the laws under which private corporations are formed, the State cannot exercise any control over the property of a corporation, except such as may be exercised through control over its franchise, and over like property of natural persons engaged in similar business.

9. The proceeding for the assessment of property—that is, the ascertainment of its value upon evidence taken—is judicial in its character ; and to its validity the law authorizing it must provide some kind of notice, and an opportunity to be heard respecting it, before the proceeding

becomes final; or it will want the essential ingredient of due process of law. The notice may be given by personal citation or by statute. It is usually given by a statute prescribing a time and place where parties may be heard before boards appointed for the correction of errors in assessment.

10. The Constitution of California (section 15, article IV.) provides that "on the final passage of all bills they shall be read at length, and the vote shall be by yeas and nays upon each bill separately, and shall be entered on the journal, and no bill shall become a law without the concurrence of a majority of the members elected to each house." Under this provision, the Court, to inform itself, will look to the journals of the Legislature, and if it appears therefrom that the bill did not pass by the constitutional majority, then it will not be regarded as a law. SAWYER, J.

11. The journals of the Legislature show that the Act of March 14, 1881, mentioned in the opinion, never became a law. SAWYER, J.

12. Where the original written journals on file in the office of the Secretary of State differ in any material particular from the printed journals, the original written journals are the authentic official records, and must control. SAWYER, J.

Counsel for Plaintiffs :—
    E. C. MARSHALL, Att'y-Gen. of California,
    D. M. DELMAS,
    D. S. TERRY,
    A. L. RHODES,
    W. T. BAGGETT,
    J. H. CAMPBELL, Dist. Att'y of Santa Clara Co.,
    J. T. CAREY, Dist. Att'y of Sacramento Co., and
    J. M. LESSER, Dist. Att'y of Santa Cruz Co.

Counsel for Defendants :—
    S. W. SANDERSON,
    J. N. POMEROY,
    T. I. BERGIN,
    H. S. BROWN,
    S. C. DENSON, and
    P. D. WIGGINGTON.

OPINION OF THE COURT.

By the Court: FIELD, *Circuit Justice:*

These are actions for the recovery of unpaid State and County Taxes levied upon certain property of the several defendants, either for the fiscal year of 1881 or of 1882, and alleged to be due to the plaintiffs, with an additional five per cent., as a penalty for their non-payment, and interest. The defendants are corporations formed under the laws of California, and the taxes claimed were levied on the franchise, roadway, roadbed, rails and rolling-stock of each of them as an unit, without separation or distinction in the valuation of the different parts composing the whole. To two of the corporations, the Southern Pacific Railroad Company and the Central Pacific Railroad Company, privileges and powers, other than those acquired under the laws of the State, were conferred by grant of the General Government; and for them obligations and burdens were assumed not contemplated nor possible under their original organization.

It is contended that Congress has selected these corporations as the special agents and instruments of the nation for public purposes, and to that end has clothed them with faculties, powers and privileges to enable them to construct and maintain their roads as postal and military roads of the Government; that the State by an act of its Legislature has assented to the acceptance of these faculties, powers and privileges, and that the companies in consideration thereof have assumed obligations to the General

Government with the discharge of which the State cannot interfere; that the power to tax their franchises involves the power to destroy the companies and thus deprive the General Government of the benefit of the roads, for the construction and maintenance of which its grants were made; that the existence and exercise of the power on the part of the State are therefore incompatible with the duties devolved upon and assumed by the companies to the United States. Hence it is claimed by counsel that the tax levied upon the franchises of the defendants is illegal and void; and they refer to numerous decisions of the Supreme Court which hold, in general language, that an agency of the United States, an instrumentality by which the Federal Government discharges its obligations to the people of the country, cannot be taxed by any State or subordinate authority. Certainly no State can impede or embarrass the Federal Government in its operations, as might be done if it could impose a tax upon the necessary means adopted for their execution; nor can the Federal Government impede or embarrass the operations of the State governments, as it might do, if it could impose a tax upon the necessary means adopted by them in the exercise of their powers.

The two governments have supreme authority within their respective spheres, and within them neither can inter fere with the other. On this principle it was held by the Supreme Court that the State could not levy a tax upon the salary or emoluments of an officer of the United States; nor could the United States impose a tax upon the salary of a State Judge. (*Dobbins* vs. *Commissioners of Erie County*, 16 Peters, 435; *Collector* vs. *Day*, 11 Wall., 113.) Both officers were necessary agents, instrumentalities for exercising the powers of their respective governments, and to tax the salary of either was to impair the means by which he could exist and maintain his office. In both cases, as observed by Mr. Justice Nelson, the exemption from taxation was "upheld by the great law of self-preservation, as any government whose means employed in conducting its operations is subject to the control of another, can exist only at the mercy of that government." The correctness of this general principle is not controverted, and cannot be in the face of the numerous decisions of the Supreme Court, when applied to the means or instrumentalities created by the Federal Government, or existing under its laws, for the exercise of its powers, such as officers of its Courts in the administration of justice, or fiscal agents in the collection, custody, or distribution of its funds. But we are unable to accede to the position that every agent or instrument which the United States may see fit to employ, is thereby exempted from the common burdens of the State in which it may be found or used, in the absence of specific Congressional legislation declaring such exemption. The coach employed to carry the mail, or the ferry-boat to convey it across a navigable stream, would hardly, by reason of this employment alone as an instrumentality of the General Government, be considered as withdrawn from the taxing power of the State. As well observed by Chief Justice Chase, with reference to the exemption from State taxation claimed by the Kansas Division of the Pacific Railroad Company for its property, no limits can be perceived to the principle of exemption which the companies thus seek to establish. "Every corporation," he added, "engaged in the transportation of mails, or of Government property of any description, by land or water, or in supplying materials for the use of the Government, or in performing any service of whatever kind, might claim the benefit of the exemption. The amount of property now held by such corporations, and having relations more or less direct to the National Government and its service, is very great. And this amount is continually increasing; so that it may admit of question whether the whole income of the property which will

2

remain liable to State taxation, if the principle contended for is admitted and applied in its fullest extent, may not ultimately be found inadequate to the support of the State governments." (*Thomson* vs. *Pacific Railroad*, 9 Wall., 579, 591.)

It is true, that in the case from which this citation is made, exemption from taxation was claimed only for the property, the road and rolling-stock of the Company. Here the exemption claimed is of the franchises of the corporations, their right to exist and maintain their roads. But it is not perceived that this difference between the cases can affect the rule which was there laid down, that unless Congress interposes and creates the exemption, the taxing power of the State is not restrained; for if the roads and rolling-stock can be taxed, and, if the taxes are not paid, can be sold, the ability of the companies to discharge their obligations as agents of the Government, would be as effectually destroyed, as by the taxation and sale of their franchises. The possession of the roads and rolling-stock is as essential as the possession of the franchises.

The objection presented by counsel is not free from difficulty. At one time I thought that it was tenable, and so expressed myself by joining in the dissent in *Railroad Company* vs. *Peniston*, reported in 18 Wallace; but on further consideration, I have come to the conclusion that the rule laid down in *Thomson's Case* is the true and sound rule. The State, it is conceded, cannot use its taxing power so as to defeat or burden the operations of the General Government; and when that Government has itself created the instrumentality used, its exemption from State taxation necessarily follows. But we are of opinion, yielding to the decision cited, that when the instrumentality is the creation of the State—a corporation formed under its laws—and is employed or adopted by the General Government for its convenience, although to enlarge its use and render it more available additional privileges and benefits are conferred by that Government upon the corporation, it remains subject to the taxing power of the State, unless Congress declares it to be exempt from such power. Congress can undoubtedly exempt any agencies it may employ for services to the General Government from such taxation as will in its judgment impede or prevent their performance. Occasions may arise hereafter, especially in time of war, where the necessities of the Federal Government will require such exemption of the roads of the companies and of their franchises and appurtenances to be declared and enforced, the exemption to continue until the necessities calling for it shall cease. But as yet Congress has not declared any such exemption either of their property or of their franchises; and we therefore think that none exists.

Of the other defences interposed to the claim of the plaintiffs, some are founded upon an alleged neglect of the assessing officers to comply with the requirements of the laws of the State, and some upon the alleged conflict of provisions of the State Constitution, under which they acted, with requirements of the Federal Constitution. Of the former are objections to what is termed the lumping character of the assessment, that is, the blending of the different items composing the whole into one valuation, namely, the value of the franchise, roadway, roadbed, rails and rolling-stock, without any designation of the value of each distinct part; and to the including in the roadway of property not properly appertaining to it, such as fences on its sides belonging to adjoining proprietors; and, so far as the roadway of the Central Pacific Company is concerned, to the including in the estimate of its length the four miles of the bay between the road in the county of San Francisco and the wharf in Alameda County. The value of the fences is included in the valuation of the roadway of each company. The distance across the bay of San Francisco is added to the length of the road assessed to the Central Pacific Company, and is assessed as of equal value per

mile with the rest of the road. It is also contended that
the land composing the roadway, and the rails laid thereon,
should have been separately assessed; the latter as improvements under the Constitution of the State, which requires
"land and improvements thereon" to be separately assessed. An objection is also taken to those cases in which
the people of the State are plaintiffs, that the statute under which they were brought was repealed in 1880, and
that after that period actions for unpaid taxes could be
brought only in the name of the county. We do not,
however, deem it important to pass upon these and other
objections to the assessment, arising from an alleged disregard of the laws of the State. We shall confine ourselves
to the defences made to the assessment and tax from the
alleged conflict of the provisions, under which they were
levied, with the requirements of the Fourteenth Amendment to the Constitution of the United States, which declares that no State shall "deprive any person of life,
liberty, or property without due process of law, nor deny to
any person within its jurisdiction the equal protection of
the laws." The railroad companies contend that both inhibitions of this amendment were violated in the assessment and taxation of their property.

The Constitution of California provides for taxes on
property, on incomes, and on polls. The taxation on property, with which alone we are concerned in this case, is to
be in proportion to its value. There is no provision for
levying a specific tax upon any article or kind of property.
It declares that all property, not exempt under the laws of
the United States, shall, with some exceptions, be taxed
according to its value, to be ascertained as prescribed by
law; and that the word "property" shall "include moneys,
credits, bonds, stocks, dues, franchises, and all other matters
and things, real, personal, and mixed, capable of private
ownership."

It also declares that a "mortgage, deed of trust, contract, or other obligation by which a debt is secured, *shall,*

for the purposes of assessment and taxation, be deemed and treated as an interest in the property affected thereby." And that, "*except as to railroads and other quasi public corporations,* in case of debts so secured, the value of the property affected by such mortgage, deed of trust, contract, or obligation, less the value of such security, shall be assessed and taxed to the owner of the property, and the value of such security shall be assessed and taxed to the owner thereof." It also provides that "the taxes so levied shall be a lien upon the property and security, and may be paid by either party to such security; if paid by the owner of the security, the tax so levied upon the property affected thereby shall become a part of the debt so secured; if the owner of the property shall pay the tax so levied on such security, it shall constitute a payment thereon, and to the extent of such payment a full discharge thereof."

By the Constitution not only is the *ad valorem* rule established for the taxation of property, but provision is also made for its assessment. The franchise, roadway, roadbed, rails, and rolling-stock of railroads operated in more than one county are to be assessed by a special board, termed the State Board of Equalization. All other property is to be assessed in the county in which it is situated. The Supervisors of each county are constituted a Board of Equalization of such taxable property, and must act upon prescribed rules of notice to its owners. The State Board is authorized to act not only as assessor of the franchise, roadway, roadbed, rails, and rolling-stock of the railroads mentioned, but as a Board of Equalization of the taxable property in the several counties, so that equality may be secured between the tax-payers of different localities. Its action in this latter character must also be upon prescribed rules of notice. But though the officers by whom the assessment of these properties is to be made be different, the properties are subject to the same rule of taxation; that is, they are to be taxed in proportion to their value. In fixing, however, the liabilities of parties to pay the tax assessed and levied upon properties subject to a mortgage, and in estimating the value of such properties as the foundation for the tax, a discrimination is made between the property held by railroad and *quasi* public corporations, and that held by natural persons and other corporations. A mortgage, as seen by the provisions of the Constitution quoted above, is deemed and treated, for the purposes of assessment and taxation, as an interest in the property affected. At common law a mortgage of property is a conveyance of the title, subject to a condition that if the debt secured be paid as stipulated the conveyance is to become inoperative. Until the debt secured is paid, the title is in the mortgagee. By the Constitution, a mortgage, for the purposes of assessment and taxation, operates in like manner to transfer the mortgagor's interest to the extent represented by the amount secured. If such amount be half the value of the property, the taxable interest of the mortgagee is an undivided half interest in the property; if the amount equal or exceed the whole value of the property, the taxable interest of the mortgagee embraces the entire property. The value of the security can never exceed the value of the property mortgaged; it may be less, and is so if the amount secured be less than such value.

Now, under the Constitution, when, by the execution of a mortgage, a taxable interest in the property held by natural persons or by corporations other than railroad or *quasi* public, is transferred by the owner to another party, or the whole taxable interest is vested in him, the holder alone of such interest is taxed for it. It is assessed against him as the owner of it, and against him alone could it be justly assessed. But when, by a mortgage on the property of a railroad or a *quasi* public corporation, a taxable interest in such property is transferred by the corporation to another, or the whole interest is vested in him, the holder of such interest is exempted from taxation for it, and the corporation is assessed and taxed for it, notwithstanding the transfer. No account is taken of the transfer of the taxable interest in the estimate of the value of the property. It is still assessed and taxed to the original holder. The discrimination thus made will more clearly appear by an illustration of the practical operation of the provisions. If, for example, A, owning property worth $20,-000, should execute a mortgage thereof to the Nevada Bank, in San Francisco, to secure $10,000, the bank would hold a taxable interest in that property to the amount of an undivided half. Its liability for taxation would be precisely as though an absolute conveyance of an undivided half interest had been made to it. And the Constitution, as seen above, requires that each owner shall pay the tax on his separate interest; and if he pay the tax chargeable on the interest of the other, he shall be allowed for it, either by an addition to the mortgage debt, or a discharge of a portion of that debt according as he is the one or the other party to the security. No one would pretend that the mortgagor should pay without such allowance the tax chargeable to the bank, nor that the bank should pay the tax chargeable to the mortgagor, except upon like condition. It would be difficult to state any principle which would justify the exaction from one of a tax leviable on the interest of the other. No power in any State has ever been asserted going to that extent, except the power to confiscate. The exaction would not be the taking of property by due process of law, even upon the theories as to what constitutes such process asserted in this case; it would be sheer spoliation by arbitrary power.

If, however, a railroad corporation should execute its mortgage to the Nevada Bank to secure a loan equal to half or the whole of the value of its property, and thus transfer to the bank a portion or the whole of its taxable interest in the property, that which is thus condemned as sheer spoliation would be enforced, if effect be given to the Constitution as it is written. The taxable interest in that case held by the bank would not be assessed nor taxed to the bank. If the mortgage should be for half of the value of the property, the railroad company would still have to pay the tax on the interest transferred, and would not be allowed any credit on the mortgage for the amount paid. If the mortgage should be equal to or exceed the whole value of the property, the railroad company, which would not in such a case hold any taxable interest in the property—no more than if it had been previously transferred by an absolute conveyance—would still be required to pay the tax upon it, and without any credit for the payment. On what principle, or by what species of reasoning a tax upon property can be upheld and enforced against a party, be the party a natural or an artificial person, when the taxable interest in it had, at the time of the levy of the tax, been transferred to another, I am at a loss to understand. This position of the case was suggested to counsel on more than one occasion during the argument; but no answer was made to it. To every other position an answer was attempted, but to this one none; and, as we think, for the best of reasons, because none was possible, unless indeed it be held that the Constitution does not mean what in express language it declares, that a mortgage " *shall for the purposes of assessment and taxation be deemed and treated as an interest in the property affected thereby.*"

Under the provisions of the Constitution cited, the property of the several railroad companies, defendants in these cases, was assessed and taxed; and in such assessment and taxation, all the injurious discriminations mentioned were applied against the companies, as will appear by a statement of the proceedings. In considering them, it will tend to clearness and brevity, if we confine what we have to say principally to the case of Santa Clara County against the Southern Pacific Railroad Company. The circumstances distinguishing the other cases from it do not affect the questions involved.

The Southern Pacific Railroad Company operates a railroad through several counties. The entire length of the road is somewhat over 711 miles, of which 59 miles and three-tenths of a mile are in the county of Santa Clara. The principal place of business of the company is in the city of San Francisco. Its stockholders are citizens of the United States, some of whom reside in California and some in other States. On the 1st of April, 1875, it was indebted to divers persons in large sums of money advanced for the construction and equipment of its road; and to secure this indebtedness and to complete the construction and equipment, it executed and delivered to certain parties, D. O. Mills and Lloyd Tevis, of the city and county of San Francisco, a mortgage upon its road, franchises, rolling-stock and appurtenances, and upon a large number of tracts of land, situated in different counties, aggregating over 11,000,000 acres, which were the property of the company. The indebtedness amounted to the sum of $32,520,000, and consisted of various bonds of the company. A portion of these bonds, amounting to about $1,632,000, has been paid; and so has the accruing interest on all of them. The balance of the bonds, amounting to about $30,898,000, remains a subsisting indebtedness. This mortgage was soon afterwards placed on record in the office of the Recorder of Deeds in the several counties of the State in which the property is situated.

The State Board of Equalization assessed the franchise, roadway, roadbed, rails, and rolling-stock of that portion of the road which is designated as its Main Branch, being $160\frac{84}{100}$ miles in length, at $2,412,600, making $15,000 a mile, and apportioned to the county of Santa Clara $889,-500. Upon this amount thus assessed and apportioned, the taxes were levied for which the action of that county is brought. Another portion of the road, designated as the Southern Division, was assessed in a similar manner, and the amount apportioned to the different counties through which the road passed. In making the assessment of the different portions, no deduction was allowed for the mortgage thereon. No account was taken of the mortgage; it was not treated as an interest in the property, nor as affecting in any way the liability of the mortgagor for the tax. If a natural person had executed the mortgage, it being for an amount exceeding the value of the property, the whole taxable interest would have been treated as in the mortgagees, and they alone would have been assessed and taxed; they alone would have been held amenable to a personal action for the taxes. If the mortgagor had paid the taxes to prevent a sale of the property, the amount paid would have been credited on the mortgage. It can hardly require further illustration to show the discrimination against railroad companies in the matter of taxation, where property is subject to a mortgage. Not only is the company taxed in such a case for interests it does not possess, but it is not allowed any credit by those who do possess the interests for the amount exacted.

The same discrimination will appear against railroad companies in the taxation of their property, if we treat mortgages thereon, not as *interests* in the property, which the Constitution declares they shall be deemed and treated to be, but as mere liens or incumbrances thereon. The basis of all *ad valorem* taxation is necessarily the assessment of the property, that is, the estimate of its value. Whatever affects the value necessarily increases or diminishes the tax proportionately. If, therefore, any element which is taken into consideration in the valuation of the property of one party be omitted in the valuation of the property of another, a discrimination is made against the one and in favor of the other, which destroys the uniformity so essential to all just and equal taxation. Such an element exists where in the assessment of property subject to a mortgage, the value of the mortgage is deducted if the property be owned by a natural person, and is not deducted if owned by a railroad corporation. And the Constitution of the State declares that in the ascertainment of values as the basis of taxation such deduction shall be allowed in the one case and denied in the other. Instances of every-day occurrence will show the effect of this discrimination in a clear light. A natural person and a railroad company own together a parcel of property in equal proportions subject to a mortgage. In estimating the value of the undivided half belonging to the natural person, half of the amount of the mortgage is deducted. In estimating the value of the undivided half belonging to the railroad company, no part of the mortgage is deducted. The discrimination is made against the company, for no other reason than its ownership. Take another instance: a natural person and a railroad company own tracts of land adjoining each other, of the same quantity and of equal fertility and richness, both being subject to a mortgage. In the estimate of the value of the property belonging to the natural person the amount of the mortgage is deducted; in the estimate of the value of the property belonging to the railroad company the mortgage is not deducted. Of course, the valuation of the latter, and consequent tax is proportionately increased; and this discrimination is made solely because of the ownership of the property. Should these two owners exchange their lands, the valuation made would change with the ownership. Should the railroad company sell its tract to an individual, the assessing officers would at once be bound to return a different valuation of the property as a basis for taxation. Every one sees that the valuation has not in fact changed with the ownership, and, therefore, that the discrimination is made solely because a rule is adopted in the assessment of the property of one party different from that applied in the assessment of the property of the other, purely on account of its ownership. A corresponding difference in the tax which the different owners must pay follows the assessment. Thus, if two adjoining tracts are subject to a mortgage each for half its value, the natural person owning one of them pays a tax on the other half, while the corporation must pay a tax on the whole of its tract, that is, double the tax of the individual. Thus, if each tract be worth $100,000, subject to a mortgage of $50,000, and the rate of taxation be two per cent., the tax of the individual will be $1,000; the tax of the corporation will be $2,000. If, then, these owners should exchange their lands, the property which this year is thus taxed at $1,000, will next year be taxed at double the amount; and the other tract, this year taxed at $2,000, will next year be taxed at one-half that sum. The property which is now half exempt will then be subject to taxation to its full value; and that which is now taxable at its full value will then be half exempt; and all this change in valuation without any change in the character or use of the property, but solely on account of the change in its ownership.

The principle which sanctions the elimination of one element in assessing the value of property held by one party, and takes it into consideration in assessing the value of property held by another party, would sanction the assessment of the property of one at less than its value— at a half or a quarter of it—and the property of another at more than its value—at double or treble of it—according to the will or caprice of the State. To-day, railroad companies are under its ban, and the discrimination is against their property. To-morrow, it may be that other institutions will incur its displeasure. If the property of railroad companies may be thus sought out and subjected to discriminating taxation, so, at the will of the State by a change of its Constitution, may the property of churches, of universities, of asylums, of savings banks, of insurance companies, of rolling and flouring mill companies, of mining companies, indeed of any corporate companies existing in the State. The principle which justifies such a discrimination in assessment and taxation, where one of the owners is a railroad corporation and the other a natural person, would also sustain it where both owners are natural persons. A mere change in the State Constitution would effect this if the Federal Constitution does not forbid it. Any difference between the owners, whether of age, color, or race, or sex, which the State might designate would be a sufficient reason for the discrimination. It would be a singular comment upon the weakness and character of our republican institutions, if the valuation and consequent taxation of property could vary according as the owner is white, or black, or yellow, or old, or young, or male, or female. A classification of values for taxation upon any such ground would be abhorrent to all notions of equality of right among men. Strangely indeed would the law sound in case it read that in the assessment and taxation of property, a deduction should be made for mortgages thereon if the property be owned by white men or by old men, and not deducted if owned by black men or by young men; deducted if owned by landsmen, not deducted if owned by sailors; deducted if owned by married men, not deducted if owned by bachelors; deducted if owned by men doing business alone, not deducted if owned by men doing business in partnerships or other associations; deducted if owned by trading corporations, not deducted if owned by churches or universities; and so on, making a discrimination whenever there was any difference in the character, or pursuit, or condition of the owner. To levy taxes upon a valuation of property thus made is of the very essence of tyranny, and has never been done except by bad governments in evil times, exercising arbitrary and despotic power.

Until the adoption of the Fourteenth Amendment, there was no restraint to be found in the Constitution of the United States against the exercise of such power by the States. In many particulars the States were previously limited; their sovereignty was a restricted one. They could not declare war, nor make treaties of peace. They could not enter into compacts with each other. They could not pass a bill of attainder, nor an *ex post facto* law, nor a law impairing the obligation of contracts. They could not interfere with the exercise of the powers, nor obstruct the laws of the Federal Government. But in many other particulars the power of the States was supreme, subject to no control by the Constitution of the United States. The original amendments were only limitations upon the Federal Government, and did not affect the States. Among the powers still held by the States was the power of taxation. When not interfering with any power or purpose or agent of the Federal Government, there was no limitation upon its exercise. Except as restrained by their own Constitutions, the States might impose taxes upon any property within their jurisdiction, and, as said in the *Delaware Tax Case* (18 Wall., 231), the manner in which its value was assessed and the rate of taxation, however arbitrary or capricious, were mere matters of legislative discretion; and it was not for the Court to suggest in any case that a more equitable mode of assessment or rate of taxation might be adopted than the one prescribed by the Legislature of the State.

The first section of the Fourteenth Amendment places a limit upon all the powers of the State, including among others that of taxation. After stating that all persons born or naturalized in the United States, and subject to the jurisdiction thereof, are citizens of the United States and of the State in which they reside, it declares that " no State shall make or enforce any law which shall abridge the privileges or immunities of citizens of the United States; nor shall any State deprive any *person* (dropping the designation citizen) of life, liberty, or property without due process of law, nor deny to any person within its jurisdiction the equal protection of the laws." The amendment was adopted soon after the close of the civil war, and undoubtedly had its origin in a purpose to secure the newly made citizens in the full enjoyment of their freedom. But it is in no respect limited in its operation to them. It is universal in its application, extending its protective force over all men of every race and color, within the jurisdiction of the States throughout the

broad domain of the Repnblic. A constitutional provision is not to be restricted in its application because
designed originally to prevent an existing wrong. Such
a restricted interpretation was urged in the *Dartmouth
College Case*, to prevent the application of the provision
prohibiting legislation by States impairing the obligation
of contracts to the charter of the college, it being contended that the charter was not such a contract as the prohibition contemplated. Chief Justice Marshall, however,
after observing that it was more than possible that the pres-
ervation of rights of that description was not particularly
in view of the framers of the Constitution when that clause
was introduced, said: "It is not enough to say that this
particular case was not in the mind of the convention
when the article was framed, nor of the American people
when it was adopted. It is necessary to go further, and
to say that, had this particular case been suggested, the
language would have been so varied as to exclude it, or it
would have been made a special exception. The case
being within the words of the rule, must be within its operation likewise, unless there be something in the literal
construction so obviously absurd or mischievous, or repug-
nant to the general spirit of the instrument, as to justify
those who expound the Constitution in making it an exception." (4 Wheat., 494.) All history shows that a particular grievance suffered by an individual or a class, from
a defective or oppressive law, or the absence of any law
touching the matter, is often the occasion and cause for
enactments, constitutional or legislative, general in their
character, designed to cover cases not merely of the same,
but all cases of a similar nature. The wrongs which were
supposed to be inflicted upon or threatened to citizens of
the enfranchised race, by special legislation directed
against them, moved the framers of the amendment to
place in the fundamental law of the nation provisions not
merely for the security of those citizens, but to insure to all
men, at all times and at all places, due process of law, and

the equal protection of the laws. Oppression of the person and spoliation of property by any State were thus forbidden, and equality before the law was secured to all. In the argument of the *San Mateo Case* in the Supreme Court, Mr. Edmunds, who was a member of the Senate when the amendment was discussed and adopted by that body, speaking of its broad and catholic spirit, said: "There is no word in it that did not undergo the completest scrutiny. There is no word in it that was not scanned, and intended to mean the full and beneficial thing that it seems to mean. There was no discussion omitted; there was no conceivable posture of affairs to the people who had it in hand," which was not considered. And the purpose of this long and anxious consideration was that protection against injustice and oppression should be made forever secure—to use his language—"secure, not according to the passion of Vermont, or of Rhode Island, or of California, depending upon their local tribunals for its efficient exercise—but secure as the right of a Roman was secure, in every province and in every place, and secure by the judicial power, the legislative power, and the executive power of the whole body of the States and the whole body of the people."

With the adoption of the amendment the power of the States to oppress any one under any pretence, or in any form, was forever ended; and henceforth all persons within their jurisdiction could claim equal protection under the laws. And by equal protection is meant equal security to every one in his private rights—in his right to life, to liberty, to property, and to the pursuit of happiness. It implies not only that the means which the laws afford for such security shall be equally accessible to him, but that no one shall be subject to any greater burdens or charges than such as are imposed upon all others under like circumstances. This protection attends every one everywhere, whatever be his position in society or his association with others, either for profit, improvement, or pleasure. It does not leave him because of any social or official position which he may hold, nor because he may belong to a political body, or to a religious society, or be a member of a commercial, manufacturing, or transportation company. It is the shield which the arm of our blessed Government holds at all times over every one, man, woman, and child, in all its broad domain, wherever they may go and in whatever relations they may be placed. No State—such is the sovereign command of the whole people of the United States—no State shall touch the life, the liberty, or the property of any person, however humble his lot or exalted his station, without due process of law; and no State, even with due process of law, shall deny to any one within its jurisdiction the equal protection of the laws.

Unequal taxation, so far as it can be prevented, is, therefore, with other unequal burdens, prohibited by the amendment. There undoubtedly are, and always will be, more or less inequalities in the operation of all general legislation, arising from the different conditions of persons, from their means, business, or position in life, against which no foresight can guard. But this is a very different thing, both in purpose and effect, from a carefully devised scheme to produce such inequality; or a scheme, if not so devised, necessarily producing that result. Absolute equality may not be attainable, but gross and designed departures from it will necessarily bring the legislation authorizing it within the prohibition. The amendment is aimed against the perpetration of injustice, and the exercise of arbitrary power to that end. The position that unequal taxation is not within the scope of its prohibitory clause would give to it a singular meaning. It is a matter of history that unequal and discriminating taxation levelled against special classes, has been the fruitful means of oppressions, and the cause of more commotions and disturbance in society, of insurrections and revolutions, than any other cause in the world. It would, indeed, as counsel in

3

the *San Mateo Case* ironically observed, be a charming spectacle to present to the civilized world, if the amendment were to read as contended it does in law—"Nor shall any State deprive any person of his property without due process of law, *except it be in the form of taxation*—nor deny to any person within its jurisdiction the equal protection of the laws, *except it be by taxation*" No such limitation can be thus engrafted by implication upon the broad and comprehensive language used. The power of oppression by taxation without due process of law is not thus permitted; nor the power by taxation to deprive any person of the equal protection of the laws.

Soon after the adoption of the amendment, Congress recognized by its legislation the application of the prohibition to unequal taxation. The original Civil Rights Act, previously passed, made persons of the emancipated race citizens, and declared that all citizens of the United States of every race or color should have the same rights in every State and Territory to make and enforce contracts, to sue, be parties, and give evidence; to inherit, purchase, lease, sell, own, and convey real and personal property, and to the benefit of all laws and proceedings for the security of persons and property, as was enjoyed by white citizens, and should be subject to like punishments, pains and penalties, and to none other. After the adoption of the amendment the act was re-enacted, and to the clause that all persons should enjoy the same rights as white citizens, and be subject to like punishments, pains and penalties, it added and subject only to like "*taxes, licenses, and exactions of every kind, and to no other.*" The Congress which re-enacted the Civil Rights Act with this addition was largely composed of those who had voted for the amendment; and it is well known that oppressions by unequal taxation were the subject of consideration before the Committee of the two Houses under whose direction the amendment was proposed. But were this otherwise, and were the wrong of such unequal taxation not prominently in the minds of the

framers, it being within the language, it must be held to
be within the operation of the prohibition. As truly and
eloquently said by Mr. Conkling, in the argument of the
San Mateo Case : "If it be true that new needs have come,
if it be true that wrongs have arisen or shall arise which
the framers in their forebodings never saw; wrongs which
shall be righted by the words they established;. then all the
more will those words be sanctified and consecrated to hu-
manity and progress."

The fact to which counsel allude, that certain property
is often exempted from taxation by the States, does not
at all militate against this view of the operation of the
Fourteenth Amendment in forbidding the imposition of
unequal burdens. Undoubtedly since the adoption of
that amendment the power of exemption is much more
restricted than formerly—but that it may be extended
to property used for objects of a public nature, is not
questioned—that is, where the property is used for the
promotion of the public well-being, and not for any
private end. Thus property used for public instruction,
for schools, colleges, and universities, which are open to
all applicants on similar conditions, may properly be exempted. The public benefit is the equivalent to the
State for the tax which would otherwise be exacted. If
buildings, used as churches for public worship, are also
sometimes exempted, it must be because, apart from religious considerations, churches are regarded as institutions
established to inculcate principles of sound morality, lead-
ing citizens to a more ready obedience to the laws.
Whatever the exemption, it can only be sustained for the
public service or benefit received. The equality of protec
tion which the Fourteenth Amendment declares that no
State shall deny to any one is not thus invaded. That
amendment requires that exactions upon property for the
public shall be levied according to some common ratio to
its value, so that each owner may contribute only his just
proportion to the general fund. When such exaction is

made without reference to a common ratio, it is not a tax, whatever else it may be termed; it is rather a forced contribution, amounting in fact to simple confiscation. As justly said by the Supreme Court of Kentucky, in the celebrated case of *Lexington* vs. *McQuillan's Heirs*, whenever the property of a citizen is taken from him by the sovereign will and appropriated without his consent to the benefit of the public, the exaction should not be considered as a tax unless similar contributions be exacted by the same public will from such members of the same community as own the same kind of property; and, although there may be a discrimination in the subjects of taxation, still persons of the same class and property of the same kind must generally be subjected alike to the same common burden. (9 Dana, Ky., 513.)

The cases of *People* vs. *Weaver* (100 U. S., 539), and of *Evansville Bank* vs. *Britton* (105 id., 322), will illustrate the character of the discrimination of which the defendants complain. By an Act of Congress passed in 1864 and re-enacted in the Revised Statutes, the shares in national banks are allowed to be included in the valuation of the personal property of the owner in the assessment of taxes imposed by authority of the State in which the banks are located, subject to two restrictions; that the taxation shall not be at a greater rate than is assessed upon other moneyed capital in the hands of individual citizens of the State, and that the shares owned by non-residents of the State shall be taxed at the place where the bank is located. (R. S., sec. 5219.) In *People* vs. *Weaver*, (100 U. S., 539,) the meaning of these restrictions upon the State was considered by the Supreme Court, and it was held:

1st. That the restriction against discrimination has reference to the entire process of assessment, and includes the valuation of the shares as well as the rate of percentage charged thereon;

2d. That a statute of New York, which established a

mode of assessment by which such shares were valued higher in proportion to their real value than other moneyed capital, was in conflict with the restriction, although no greater percentage was levied on such valuation than on other moneyed capital; and,

3d. That a statute which permitted a party to deduct his just debts from the valuation of his personal property, except so much as consisted of those shares, taxed them at a greater rate than other moneyed capital, and was therefore void as to them.

The discrimination there condemned, by which an increased value was given to the shares of the national banks beyond what was given to other moneyed capital, is a discrimination similar to that made by the elimination of mortgages in estimating the value of railroad property in the cases before us. In *Evansville Bank* vs. *Britton*, the doctrine of this case is approved, and it was held that the taxation of shares in the national banks, under a statute of Indiana, without permitting the owner to deduct from their assessed value the amount of his *bona-fide* indebtedness, as he was permitted to do in the case of other investments of moneyed capital, was a discrimination forbidden by the act of Congress.

That the proceeding, by which the taxes claimed in these several actions were levied against the railroad companies on taxable interests with which they had parted, was not due process of law, seems to me so obviously true as to require no further illustration. Any additional argument would rather tend to obscure a truth which should be evident upon its simple statement. And if we assume that the mortgage in each case was a mere lien or incumbrance on the property affected, and not an interest in it, as the Constitution declares it is, then also is it clear that its elimination as an element in the valuation of the property of the defendants for taxation, while it was considered in the valuation of the property of natural persons, was a discrimination against the former, and led to unequal taxation against them. In neither view, therefore, was the assessment valid, and the taxation levied upon it cannot be sustained.

To justify these discriminating provisions and maintain the action in face of them, the plaintiffs have taken positions involving doctrines which sound strangely to those who have always supposed that the constitutional guaranties extend to all persons, whatever their relations, and protect from spoliation all property, by whomsoever held. These positions are substantially as follows: That persons cease to be within the protection of the Fourteenth Amendment, and as such entitled to the equal protection of the laws, when they become members of a corporation; that property when held by persons associated together in a corporation is subject to any disposition which the State may, at its will, see fit to make; that, in any view, the property, upon which the taxes claimed were levied, was classified by its use, taken out of its general character as real and personal property, and thus lawfully subjected to special taxation; and that the power of the State cannot be questioned by the Southern Pacific Railroad Company by reason of the covenant in its mortgage. These positions are not advanced by counsel in this language nor with the baldness here given; but they mean exactly what is here stated, or they mean nothing, as will clearly appear when we analyze the language in which they are presented.

Private corporations—and under this head, with the exception of sole corporations, with which we are not now dealing, all corporations other than those which are public are included—private corporations consist of an association of individuals united for some lawful purpose, and permitted to use a common name in their business, and have succession of membership without dissolution. As said by Chief Justice Marshall, " The great object of an incorporation is to bestow the character and properties of individuality on a collective and changing body of men." (*Providence Bank* vs. *Billings*, 4 Pet., 514, 562.) In this State they are formed under general laws. By complying with certain prescribed forms any five persons may thus associate themselves. In that sense corporations are creatures of the State; they could not exist independently of the law, and the law may, of course, prescribe any conditions, not prohibited by the Constitution of the United States, upon which they may be formed and continued. But the members do not, because of such association, lose their rights to protection, and equality of protection. They continue, notwithstanding, to possess the same right to life and liberty as before, and also to their property, except as they may have stipulated otherwise. As members of the association—of the artificial body—the intangible thing called by a name given by themselves—their interests, it is true, are undivided, and constitute only a right during the continuance of the corporation to participate in its dividends, and, on its dissolution, to a proportionate share of its assets; but it is property nevertheless, and the courts will protect it, as they will any other property, from injury or spoliation.

Whatever affects the property of the corporation, that is, of all the members united by the common name, necessarily affects their interests. If all the members of the corporation die or withdraw from the association, the corporation is dead; it lives and can live only through its members. When they disappear the corporation disappears. Whatever confiscates or imposes burdens on its property, confiscates or imposes burdens on their property; otherwise nobody would be injured by the proceeding. Whatever advances the prosperity or wealth of the corporation, advances proportionately the prosperity and business of the corporators; otherwise no one would be benefited. It is impossible to conceive of a corporation suffering an injury or reaping a benefit except through its members. The legal entity, the metaphysical being that is called a corporation, cannot feel either. So, therefore, whenever a provision of the Constitution or of a law guarantees to persons protection in their property or affords to them the means for its protection, or prohibits injurious legislation affecting it, the benefits of the provision or law are extended to corporations, not to the name under which different persons are united, but to the individuals composing the union. The courts will always look through the name to see and protect those whom the name represents. Thus, inasmuch as the Constitution extended the judicial power of the United States to controversies between citizens of a State and aliens, and between citizens of different States, because its framers apprehended that State tribunals in such controversies might be swayed by local feelings, prejudices, or attachments, Chief Justice Marshal, speaking for the whole Supreme Court, held that corporations were within the provision. "Aliens, or citizens of different States," said that great judge, "are not less susceptible of these apprehensions, nor can they be supposed to be less the objects of constitutional provision, because they are allowed to sue by a corporate name. That name, indeed, cannot be an alien or a citizen, but the persons whom it represents may be the one or the other; and the controversy is, in fact and in law, between these persons suing in their corporate character, by their corporate name, for a corporate right, and the individual against whom the suit may be instituted. Substantially and essentially, the parties in such a case, where the members of the corporation are aliens or citizens of a different State from the opposite party, come within the spirit and terms of the jurisdiction conferred by the Constitution on the national tribunals. Such has been the universal understanding on the subject." (*The United States* vs. *Devaux*, 5 Cranch, 61, 87.)

Similar was the construction given by that court to a clause in the treaty of peace of 1783 between the United States and Great Britain. The sixth article provided that there should be "no future confiscation made nor any prosecutions commenced against any person or persons for or by reason of the part which he or they may have taken in the present war, and that no person shall on that account suffer any future loss or damage, either in his person, liberty or property." The State of Vermont undertook to confiscate the property of an English corporation and give it away. The corporation claimed the benefit of the article, and recovered the property against the objection that the treaty applied only to natural persons, and could not embrace corporations, because they were not persons who could have taken part in the war, or be considered British subjects. Much stronger is that case than the one now before us; but the Supreme Court looked with undimmed vision through the legal entity, the artificial creation of the State, and saw the living human beings whom it represented, and protected them under their corporate name. (*Society for the Propagation of the Gospel in Foreign Parts* vs. *Town of New Haven*, 8 *Wheat.*, 464.)

The Fifth Amendment to the Constitution declares that no person shall " be deprived of life, liberty, or property, without due process of law." This is a limitation upon the Federal Government similar to that which exists in the Constitution of several of the States against their own legislative bodies; and the term person thus used has always been held, either by tacit assent or express adjudication, whenever the question has arisen, to extend, so far as property is concerned, to corporations; because to protect them from spoliation is to protect the corporators also.

Now, the Fourteenth Amendment extends in this respect the same prohibition to the States that the Fifth Amendment did to the Federal Government—" Nor shall any State deprive any person of life, liberty, or property without due process of law "—and it adds to the inhibition, " nor deny to any person within its jurisdiction the equal protection of the laws." By every canon of construction known to the jurisprudence of the country, the same meaning must be given to the term person in the latter provision as in the former. Surely these great constitutional provisions, which have been, not inaptly, termed a new *Magna Charta*, cannot be made to read, as counsel contend; "Nor shall any State deprive any person of life, liberty, or property without due process of law, *unless he be associated with others in a corporation*, nor deny to any person within its jurisdiction the equal protection of the laws, *unless he be a member of a corporation.*" How petty and narrow would provisions thus limited appear in the fundamental law of a great people!

The constitutional guaranties of due process of law and of equality before the law would be dwarfed into comparative insignificance, and almost emasculated of their protective force, if restricted in their meaning and operation, as contended by counsel. A large proportion of our people are members of some corporation—religious, educational, scientific, trading, manufacturing, or commercial—and the amount of property held by them embraces the greater part of the wealth of the country. According to the report of the Commissioner of Railroads, made to the Secretary of the Interior, for the year ending June 30, 1882, the railroad companies operated that year 104,813 miles of railway, and transported 350 million tons of freight, of the estimated value of 12,000 million dollars. The value of these roads alone was 2,600 million dollars, and they employed that year 1,200,000 persons in operating the roads, besides 400,000 in construction—a total of 1,600,000 persons—about one thirty-third part of our population estimated at 53,000,000.*

The value of the property of manufacturing companies is over 1,000 million dollars; of national banks, over 700 millions; of insurance companies, over 600 millions; of mining companies, over 300 millions; and of telegraph companies and shipping companies, each over 100 million

---

* These figures are taken by the Commissioner from the estimate of Henry V. Poor, a compiler of railroad statistics.

dollars. Indeed, the aggregate wealth of all the trading, commercial, manufacturing, mining, shipping, transportation and other companies engaged in business, or formed for religious, educational, or scientific purposes, amounts to billions upon billions of dollars—and yet all this vast property, which keeps our industries flourishing, and furnishes employment, comforts, and luxuries to all classes, and thus promotes civilization and progress, is lifted, according to the argument of counsel, out of the protection of the constitutional guaranties, by reason of the incorporation of the companies—that is, because the persons composing them, amounting in the aggregate to nearly half the entire population of the country, have united themselves in that form under the law for the convenience of business. If the property for that reason is exempted from the protection of one constitutional guaranty, it must be from all such guaranties. If because of it, the property can be subjected to unequal and arbitrary impositions, it may for the same reason be taken from its owners without due process of law, and taken by the State for public use without just compensation. If the position be sound, it follows that corporations hold all their property and the right to its use and enjoyment at the will of the State; that it may be invaded, seized, and the companies despoiled at the State's pleasure. It need hardly be said that there would be little security in the possession of property held by such a tenure, and of course little incentive to its acquisition and improvement.

But in truth the State possesses no such arbitrary power over the property of corporations. When allowed to acquire and own property, they must be treated as owners, with all the rights incident to ownership. They have a constitutional right to be so treated. Whatever power the State may possess in granting or in amending their charters, it cannot withdraw their property from the guaranties of the Federal Constitution. As was said in the *San Mateo Case:* "It cannot impose the condition that they shall not resort to the Courts of law for the redress of injuries or the protection of their property; that they shall make no complaint if their goods are plundered and their premises invaded; that they shall ask no indemnity if their lands be seized for public use, or be taken without due process of law; or that they shall submit without objection to unequal and oppressive burdens arbitrarily imposed upon them; that, in other words, over them and their property the State may exercise unlimited and irresponsible power. Whatever the State may do, even with the creations of its own will, it must do in subordination to the inhibitions of the Federal Constitution."

The doctrine of unlimited power of the State over corporations, their franchises and property, simply because they are created by the State, so frequently and positively affirmed by counsel, has no foundation whatever in the law of the country. By the decision of the Supreme Court of the United States in the *Dartmouth College Case*, it was settled, after great consideration, that the charter of a corporation under which its franchise—its capacity to do business and hold property—is conferred, is a contract between the corporators and the State, and, therefore, within the protection of the Federal Constitution prohibiting legislation impairing the obligation of contracts. So far from the State having unlimited control over the franchises and property of corporations, because of its paternity to them, it has under that decision only such as it possesses over the contracts and property of individuals. It cannot, from that fact alone, alter, lessen, or revoke their franchises, although they be a free gift. It cannot, from that fact alone, interfere with or impose any burdens upon their property, except as it can interfere with and impose burdens upon the property of individuals. Such is the doctrine not only of the *Dartmouth College Case*, but of an unbroken line of decisions of the Supreme Court of the United States, and of the Supreme Courts of the several States, since that case. To avoid that limitation upon their power, most of the States, in charters since granted, have reserved a right to repeal, amend, or alter them, or have inserted in their constitutions clauses reserving a right to their legislatures to repeal, alter, or amend the charters, or to repeal, alter, or amend general laws under which corporations are permitted to be formed. This reservation, in whatever form expressed, applies only to the contract of incorporation, without which it would be beyond revocation or change by the State. It removes any impediment which would otherwise exist to legislation affecting that contract. It leaves the corporation in the same position it would have occupied had the Supreme Court held in the *Dartmouth College Case* that charters are not contracts, and that laws repealing or modifying them do not impair the obligation of contracts. It accomplishes nothing more; therefore, the legislation authorized by it must relate to the contract embodied in the charter, amending, altering, or abrogating its provisions. Legislation touching any other subject is not affected by it—neither authorized nor forbidden. Its whole scope and purpose is to enable the state to pass laws with respect to the charter—the contract of incorporation—which would otherwise be in conflict with the prohibition of the Federal Constitution. Legislation dealing with the corporation in any other particular must, therefore, depend for its validity upon the same conditions which determine the validity of like legislation affecting natural persons.

The State may, of course, accompany its grant with such conditions as it may deem proper for the management of the affairs of the corporation which do not impinge upon any provision of the Federal Constitution; and by the reservation clause it will retain control over the grant and may withdraw it or modify it at pleasure. It is on this ground that the State has asserted a right to regulate the charges—the fares and freights—of corporations. But it is a novel doctrine that it can on that ground also control their property, appropriate it, burden it, and

despoil them of it, as it may choose, unrestrained by any
constitutional inhibitions. That doctrine has no standing
as yet in the law of this country. The property acquired
by corporations is held independently of any reserved
power in their charters. By force of the reservation the
State may alter, amend, or revoke what it grants; nothing
more. It does not grant the tangible and visible property of the companies, their roads, their roadways, road-
beds, rails, or rolling-stock. These are their creation or
acquisition. Over them it can exercise only such power
as may be exercised through its control of the franchises
of the companies, and such as may be exercised over
the property of natural persons engaged in similar business.

As justly said by the Supreme Court of Michigan, speaking by Mr. Justice Cooley: "It cannot be necessary at
this day to enter upon a discussion in denial of the right
of the Government to take from either individuals or corporations any property which they may rightfully have
acquired. In the most abitrary times such an act was
recognized as pure tyranny, and it has been forbidden in
England ever since *Magna Charta*, and in this country
always. It is immaterial in what way the property was
lawfully acquired, whether by labor in the ordinary voca-
tions of life, by gift or descent, or by making profitable
use of a franchise granted by the State, it is enough that
it has become private property, and it is then protected
by the law of the land." (*Detroit* vs. *Detroit and Howell
Plank Road Company*, 43 Mich., 146-7.)

But it is urged that, even with an admission of these
positions, property may be divided into classes and subjected to different rates; that such classification may be
made from inherent differences in the nature of different
parcels of property, and also from the different uses to
which the same property may be applied; and it is sought
to place the tax levied in these cases under one of these
heads. As already mentioned, the Constitution of the

State provides with respect to property that it shall be taxed in proportion to its value; it provides for no specific tax upon any article. The classification of property, either from its distinctive character or its peculiar use, must be made within the rule prescribing taxation according to value. Real and personal property differing essentially in their nature may undoubtedly be subjected to different rates; real property may be taxed at one rate, personal property at another. But in both cases the tax must bear a definite proportion to the value of the property. So, also, if use be the ground of classification, for which a different rate of taxation is prescribed, the rate must still bear a definite proportion to the value. Now, there is no difference in the rate of taxation prescribed by the law of the State for the property of railroad corporations and that prescribed for the property of individuals. There is only one rate prescribed for all property. There is, therefore, as said in the San Mateo suit, no case presented for the application of the doctrine of classification either from the peculiar character of railroad property or its use.

The ground of complaint is not that any different rate of taxation is adopted—for there is none—but that a different rule is followed in ascertaining the value of the property of railroad corporations, as a basis for taxation, from that followed in ascertaining the value of property held by natural persons. In estimating the value in one case certain elements are considered by which the value as a basis for taxation is lessened; in estimating the value in another case those elements are omitted by which the valuation is proportionately increased. All property of railroad corporations, whether used in connection with the operation of their roads or entirely distinct from any such use, is estimated without regard to any mortgages thereon, while the property of natural persons is valued with a deduction of such mortgages.

Of the property of the railroad company—the Southern Pacific—several million acres of farming lands are

included in the same mortgage which covers the roadway, roadbed, rails, and rolling-stock of the company.
No distinction is made in the assessment of the value of
any of this property because of the use of it. The whole
is assessed in the same manner without regard to the mortgage thereon; and the taxes on the whole of it thus assessed, with the exception of the taxes on the roadbed,
roadway, rails, and rolling-stock, have been paid by the
companies, or parties to whom since the levy certain parcels have been sold. The discrimination between the railroad companies and individual proprietors, in the estimate of the value of their property, is made because of
its ownership, and not from any specific differences in the
character of the property, or in the specific uses to which
it is applied.

The farming lands held by the company are not different in character from adjoining farming lands held by
natural persons, yet they are assessed under the system established by the Constitution of the State upon
different principles. The roadbed, roadway, rails, and
rolling-stock of the railroad companies, are not different
in their nature or use from the roadbed, roadway, rails,
and rolling-stock owned in many cases by natural persons,
yet they are subject to a different rule of assessment.
It is not classifying property to make a distinction of that
character in estimating its value as a basis for taxation.
It is making the amount of taxation depend, not upon the nature of the property or its use, but upon its ownership. And
if this can be done, there is no protection against unequal
and oppressive taxation. As justly observed by Mr. Edmunds in the *San Mateo Case:* " If you once concede the
point that you may classify different rates upon the values
of things, or may put up your values on different principles, as values by deduction or otherwise—which is the
same thing stated in another way—then there is no check
upon the exercise of arbitrary power. The mob or com-
mune that can get possession of the State Legislature for

one term may despoil every one of the citizens whom it chooses to despoil, and the liberty and the security of the Constitution of the United States, secured through painful exertion and great consideration, crystallized in unmistakable language—historic indeed, and beneficent as it is historic, securing national intrinsic rights everywhere and to everybody—will turn out to be an utter sham and delusion."

If to the position of counsel, that property may be classified simply because owned by a corporation, and thus differently assessed, we add the further position that the owner of the property assessed has no constitutional right to have notice of the assessment, or to be heard respecting it, though it be double or treble the value of the property—though the property be assessed at thousands, when worth only hundreds—we have a system established with a power of oppression under which no free man should ever be contented to live.

In the argument of counsel, the distinction between taxes for licenses and franchises, and taxation upon values, seems to have been overlooked; and because no notice is required in the former case, and no opportunity given to be heard, therefore it is contended that the rule is not sound, that notice is necessary, and an opportunity of being heard in the latter case where an assessment is made upon property and values are found upon evidence; yet the distinction is plain and everywhere recognized. A license tax paid by an insurance company of another State, in order to exercise its corporate powers in this State, is the consideration given for a privilege which the company may or may not take; if taken, the fee must be paid. Of course, no notice there is necessary. If a person wishes a license to do business at a particular place, or of a particular kind, such as selling liquors, cigars, clothes, or keeping a restaurant or hotel in a city, he is only to pay what the law requires and go into the business. Notice in such cases would be of no service to him, and no hearing could change

4

the result. And the state may exact the payment of a particular sum—such as it deems proper—as a condition of the grant of corporate powers, or for their continuance, and may reserve the right to alter this condition as it may choose; or rather, the State might have exercised such power and made such exaction had she not by her constitution declared that franchises should be assessed and taxed as property, according to their value. But for this provision no notice could be required of the amount demanded for the privilege granted, nor opportunity of being heard respecting it; for notice or hearing could be of no service to the company. Here we are not considering of the compensation to be paid for franchises or privileges of any kind, whether designated as taxes or license fees, but of taxation upon values. Where these are to be ascertained, and evidence is to be taken for that purpose, and a determination is to be made which is judicial in its character, there the owner must in some form—in some tribunal— have an opportunity afforded him to be heard respecting the proceeding under which his property may be taken before such proceeding becomes final and the valuation is irrevocably fixed. And in such cases there can be no valid deprivation of his property without it.

The notice to which we refer need not be a personal citation; it is sufficient if it be given by a law designating the time and place where parties may contest the justice of the valuation. As a general rule only a statutory notice is given. The State may designate the kind of notice and the manner in which it shall be given. All that we assert, or have asserted, is that there must be a notice of some kind which will call the attention of the parties to the subject, and inform them when and where they will be permitted to expose any alleged wrong in the valuation of which they may complain.

It was with reference to the class of cases, where values are to be found upon evidence, that we said in the San Mateo suit, that notice and opportunity to be heard were

essential to the validity of the assessment, and without
which the proceeding by which the tax-payer's property
was taken from him, would not be due process of law.
We have heard nothing in the argument of the present
cases or in the criticism of the authorities, which in the
slightest degree affects the accuracy of the statement. In
Stuart vs. *Palmer*, (74 N. Y., 191,) the Court of Appeals of
New York, in an elaborate opinion, speaking by Mr. Justice
Earl, said: "It is difficult to define with precision the exact
meaning and scope of the phrase 'due process of law.'
Any definition which could be given would probably fail
to comprehend all the cases to which it would apply. It
is probably better, as recently stated by Mr. Justice Mil-
ler, of the United States Supreme Court, 'to leave the
meaning to be evolved by the gradual process of judicial
inclusion and exclusion, as the cases presented for decision
shall require, with the reasoning on which such decisions
may be founded.' (*Davidson* vs. *New Orleans*, 96 U. S.,
104.) It may, however, be stated generally, that due process of law requires an orderly proceeding, adapted to the
nature of the case, in which the citizen has an opportunity
to be heard, and to defend, enforce, and protect his rights.
A hearing or an opportunity to be heard is absolutely essential. *We cannot conceive of due process of law without
this.*" And, again, "It has always been the general rule
in this country, in every system of assessment and taxation, to give the person to be assessed an opportunity to
be heard at some stage of the proceedings. That due process of law requires this has been quite uniformly recognized."

Numerous other authorities might be cited to the same
purport, and the language of Judge Cooley, in his Treatise
on Taxation, which exhibits a thoughtful consideration of
the subject, and a careful examination of the adjudged
cases, expresses the established law. Speaking of tax
cases he says: " We should say that notice of proceedings
in such cases, and an opportunity for a hearing of some

description, were matters of constitutional right. It has been customary to provide for them as a part of what is 'due process of law' for these cases, and it is not to be assumed that constitutional provisions, carefully framed for the protection of property, were intended or could be construed to sanction legislation under which officers might secretly assess one for any amount in their discretion, without giving him an opportunity to contest the justice of the assessment. It has often been very pointedly and emphatically declared that it is contrary to the first principles of justice that one should be condemned unheard, and it has also been justly observed of taxing officers, that 'it would be a dangerous precedent to hold that any absolute power resides in them to tax as they may choose without giving any notice to the owner. It is a power liable to great abuse,' and it might safely have been added, it is a power that under such circumstances would be certain to be abused. 'The general principles of law applicable to such tribunals oppose the exercise of any such power.'" (Cooley on Taxation, 266.)

The suggestion of counsel that there is a difference in the law as to notice and opportunity of being heard, where an assessment is made for local purposes and where it is made under a statute providing revenue for the State, is without foundation. Taxation for local improvements, or for city, county, or town purposes, involves the exercise of the same power which is exerted in taxation for State or general purposes. It is the sovereign power of the State in both cases which authorizes the tax, whether that power be exerted directly by an act of the Legislature, or by a municipal body as an instrumentality of the State. "That these assessments," says Cooley, speaking of such as are special, "are an exercise of the taxing power has over and over again been affirmed, until the controversy may be regarded as closed." And this statement is supported in a note to his treatise, by a reference to numerous adjudged cases. (p. 430.)

The object both of taxation for general purposes and of assessments for local purposes is to raise money. In both cases property is valued and a certain proportion of the valuation taken for the designated purpose. Whether that purpose be general or local, it in no respect changes the essential character of the proceeding. The property from which the exaction is to be made is less extensive in the one case than in the other; but in both there must be evidence of its value and a judicial determination respecting it. And the fact that in cases of local improvements there is sometimes a consideration also of the benefits to be received, takes nothing from the judicial character of the proceeding.

The clause of the Constitution which forbids deprivation of property without due process of law, places liberty under the same guaranty, and no one can be deprived of either—property or liberty—under the name of taxation, any more than under any other name, by officers of the State, without some notice of their proceedings and a right to be heard respecting their determination before it is executed.

The covenant in the mortgage of the Southern Pacific Railroad Company cannot affect one way or the other the right of the plaintiff to recover against that company. The power of the State is not enlarged nor diminished by it. It is not made with the State and could not be enforced by it. So far as the power or action of the State is concerned, it cannot possibly have any influence. It is a matter which concerns only the parties. They can by arrangement vary it any day; they may enlarge it, qualify it, or release it whenever they choose. It would be strange, indeed, if the State's power of taxation depended in any way upon the stipulation of third parties, or the validity of a tax could be affected by it. The covenant reads as follows: " And the said party of the first part hereby agrees and covenants to and with the said parties of the second part, and their successors in said trust, that·

it will pay all ordinary and extraordinary taxes, assess-ments, and other public burdens and charges which shall or may be imposed upon the property herein described and hereby mortgaged, and every part thereof." Then follows a provision that the mortgagees or any bondholder may, in case of default by the mortgagor, pay and discharge the taxes and any lien or incumbrance upon the property prior to the mortgage, and that for such payments the party making them shall be allowed interest and be secured by the mortgage.

The covenant is necessarily limited to such taxes as may be lawfully levied on the mortgaged property, such as the mortgagor is personally bound to the State to pay, and to such other liens as may arise from his previous contract with respect to the property. The mortgagor could not be required to pay any other taxes or discharge any other liens, and should the mortgagees pay or discharge any other, they could neither hold the mortgage as security for the amount, nor the mortgagor liable. The covenant cannot be construed to extend to any taxes levied in disregard of the Constitution or laws, nor to such liens as may arise from a tax on other than the mortgaged property, nor from any act of the mortgagees, nor any judgment against them. Should a judgment, for instance, against them become a lien upon all their interests in real property, and, among others, on that conferred by the mortgage, it would not be embraced by the covenant. That does not cover taxes levied or leviable on the mort-gage, nor on the bonds secured; they are not within its terms, and the State cannot enlarge its meaning.

At the time the mortgage was given, there had been conflicting decisions of the Supreme Court of the State as to the liability of mortgages to taxation. It must be supposed that the parties were well acquainted with these rulings, and, though the last decision then rendered was against their taxation, it was the subject of popular com-ment and discontent; and counsel inform us, was one of the most potent causes which led to the calling of a convention to change the Constitution. If the parties, therefore, had intended to enter into a covenant that should bind the mortgagor to pay any taxes which might thereafter be levied on the mortgage, it would have been the natural and easy way to say so. Not having said so, we cannot impute to the language used anything beyond its plain meaning—and that is, that the mortgagor would pay such taxes and discharge such liens on the property as should be legally chargeable to him; not such as the law might afterwards impose upon the mortgagees. In fact, the covenant creates no greater liability on the part of the mortgagor than would have existed without it; and it was inserted only out of abundant caution. Every mortgagor is bound to pay the taxes lawfully levied on the property mortgaged, and to discharge any liens created by his previous act; and if at any time the mortgagee is compelled to pay the taxes and discharge such liens to preserve the security, he can collect the amount from the mortgagor. So the question comes back to the original point in the case—were the taxes for which the present action was brought lawfully levied? If so, they can be enforced, whatever may be the private relations or stipulations between the parties to the security. If not lawfully levied, if the law or State Constitution, under which they were imposed, is in conflict with the inhibitions of the Federal Constitution, if the taxes were laid upon interests with which the mortgagor had parted, they cannot be enforced, whatever may be the pledges of the parties to each other. The argument of the plaintiff amounts to this—if the taxes had been lawfully levied on the mortgage, the mortgagor would have been obliged to pay them under its covenant; therefore it is not injured by the illegality of the levy, and not being injured by it, should not be heard to complain of it, but be compelled to pay the taxes. The answer to this specious reasoning is obvious. If the taxes are not lawfully·

levied, there are none for the payment of which the covenant can be invoked even by the mortgagees. The plaintiff must show that there rests upon the mortgagor a legal obligation to the State to pay the taxes, arising upon its constitution or laws, not from any stipulation the parties may have made with each other, with which the State has no concern. The action is not to enforce a lien upon the property; it is for a personal demand, and a personal liability to the State must be shown. No other liability of any kind to any party can aid a recovery.

The covenant we have been considering is not contained in the mortgage on the lands of the Central Pacific Company; and for such lands in California, amounting to upwards of six hundred and fifty thousand acres, that company is assessed and taxed without any deduction of the mortgage from their value, just as the Southern Pacific Company is taxed for its lands. The amount due on the land mortgage is over five and a 'half million dollars.

I have thus gone over, so far as I deem it necessary or important, the several positions of counsel for the plaintiffs, and in none of them do I find any sufficient answer to the objection of the defendants. This opinion might, therefore, close with a simple order directing judgment for the defendants. But owing to misapprehensions that have largely prevailed in the community since the trial of the *San Mateo Case,* which involved similar questions, as to the effect of a decision against the State upon its right to subject railroad property to its just proportion of the public burdens, I will venture to make some suggestions as to the manner in which all such demands of the State may be enforced without infringing any principle of Constitutional law. I am profoundly sensible of the irritation which a supposed desire to escape from the just burdens of government naturally creates. The more powerful, the more wealthy the party, the more intense the feeling; and it finds expression in words of bitter complaint, not merely against the party, but sometimes also against any administration of justice which tolerates such supposed evasion. It is sometimes forgotten that the Courts cannot supply the defects of the law, nor always correct the mistakes of public officers, nor the errors even of learned counsel. Certainly no member of this Court would countenance the escape of anybody from his just obligations; but it cannot, with any seeming justice, declare that one party shall discharge an obligation which the law, properly administered, would impose upon another. Its duty is to administer the law as it finds it, not to make it, never forgetting that its administration must always be in subordination to those great principles for the protection of private rights, which are embodied in our National Constitution, and which are of priceless value to every one in the State.

The railroad companies in California are taxed yearly to an amount exceeding $600,000. Their property is heavily encumbered with mortgages, amounting to much more than its actual value. Why should they not be allowed by law, if they pay this sum, a credit for it on their mortgages, as any natural person paying it would be allowed? Why should this unjust discrimination be made against them? Why should they by law be denied a credit for this more than $600,000 a year? Is there any justice in this denial? There is no difficulty in assessing and taxing the mortgages, if the words " except as to railroad and other *quasi* public corporations " be eliminated from the Constitution as invalid. The imaginary difficulty has arisen from the supposed necessity of taxing the debts, which the bonds secured. As these are held in different parts of the country, some out of the State, it would be impossible, it is said, to reach them. But the answer is that the taxes should be placed upon the mortgages, which for purposes of assessment and taxation, are to be . treated as interests in the property mortgaged, as much so as if it had been unconditionally conveyed to the mortgagees. The records of the different counties show the mortga-

.5

ges. The assessors can return to the Board of Equalization the value of the property covered by the mortgages in their respective counties, under section 3678 of the Political Code. The Board would then have the value of the property of the companies and the amount of the mortgages before them. The mortgage of the Southern Pacific Company being greater than the value of the entire mortgaged property, it would be assessed at such value. It could never, as a mortgage, be worth more than the property. If necessary or convenient, the assessment of the mortgage on the roadway, roadbed, rails, and rolling-stack could be stated separately from the value of the mortgage on other property of the company, and apportioned to the different counties as at present. The value of the mortgage on other property could also be apportioned as required by the Political Code. Why then should not this system be pursued? The State would thus collect all the taxes which it ought to collect. The tax being a lien upon the property, could be enforced by a sale of the property, just as though it was levied on the property, and not upon the mortgages. If the companies should then pay the tax, they could by the law claim credit for it on their mortgages; and it would be deducted in the payment of the interest or principal of their bonds. Then justice would be done to the corporations as it is done to individuals. The same proceeding could be pursued with the first mortgage on the property of the Central Pacific Company. That also being greater than the value of the property, the State would be able to collect as large a revenue as by taxation on the property itself, and the Company would have the benefit of the payment by a credit on its mortgage.

It follows from the views expressed, that findings must be had for the defendants, and judgment in their favor entered thereon.

CONCURRING OPINION.

SAWYER, *Circuit Judge:*

The discussion in this opinion, though applicable to all the cases tried, will have special reference to the facts in the case of Santa Clara County *vs.* The Southern Pacific Railroad Company. This case is similar in its main features to that of San Mateo *vs.* Southern Pacific Railroad Company, decided by this court last year. (8 Sawyer, 281.)

The questions involved require for their solution a construction of two clauses in the first section of the Fourteenth Amendment to the Constitution of the United States, which declare that no State shall "deprive any person of life, liberty, or property without due process of law, nor deny to any person within its jurisdiction the equal protection of the laws." Does the requirement of *due process of law* extend to the taking of property by taxation, and does equality of protection by the laws secure a person, whatever his association with others in business, from the imposition of greater burdens by taxation than such as are equally imposed upon others under like circumstances? Or, are persons excepted from the protection of these provisions when their property is taken for the support of government, or when they are associated with others in a corporation for the more convenient transaction of their business.

First. As to the meaning of the phrase, "due process of law," in the amendment, I used this language in the *San Mateo Case:* "No one, I apprehend, would for a moment contend that a man's life, or his liberty, could be legally taken away without notice of the proceeding, or without being offered an opportunity to be heard; or that a proceeding whereby his life or liberty should be forfeited, or permanently affected, without notice or opportunity to be heard in his own defence, could, by any possibility, be by 'due process of law.' In *such* cases there could be no just conception of 'due process of law,' that would not embrace these elements of notice and opportunity to be heard. Any conception excluding these elements would be abhorrent to all our ideas of either law or justice. If these elements must enter into and constitute an essential part of due process of law in respect to life and liberty, they must also constitute essential ingredients in due process of law where property is to be taken; for the guaranty in the Constitution is found in the same provision, in the same connection, and in the identical language applicable to all. One meaning, therefore, cannot be attributed to the phrase with respect to property, and another with respect to life and liberty." (Ib., 288.)

And it was argued that the same construction must be given to the same language when used in the same relation with reference to property, which is given to it when used with reference to life and liberty, and, therefore, that due process of law, whereby a party is to be deprived of his property, as one element or ingredient, must include an opportunity to be heard. This principle was conceived to be established by an unbroken line of authorities. On the trial of this case counsel have vehemently assailed this doctrine, accompanied with a confident assertion that it has *not* the sanction of any authority, and that the only authority upon the point is against it, and was not referred to by the Court or by counsel in the *San Mateo Case.* It may be well, therefore, to give some further consideration to the position asserted.

No counsel has yet appeared who has endeavored to maintain the proposition that, if a man's life is taken, or he is permanently deprived of his liberty, by some secret tribunal or body of men, without having notice or an opportunity to be heard in his own defence, he has had the benefit of " due process of law." If there is anything that was settled under the principles of the common and the constitutional law of England, before the severance of the Colonies from the mother country and the establishment of our National Constitution, it is, that no man can be deprived of his life or his liberty without being afforded an opportunity to be heard in his own defence. The law of the land—due process of law—vouchsafes to him this right or privilege. A man deprived of life without having an opportunity to be heard, is simply assassinated, or murdered; and the man permanently immured in a dungeon for an imputed offence, upon the order of any man or body of men, without an opportunity to be heard against the charge made, is arbitrarily and despotically deprived of his liberty without authority of law—without " due process of law," and in direct violation of " the law of the land." So, also, I have understood it to be equally well established, as a part of the common and constitutional law of England, as a general rule, that no man's property can be lawfully taken from him against his will without an opportunity of being heard.

The rights of life, liberty, and property are all fundamental, personal rights of the same grade or character. They are treated as such in the amendment to the Constitution in question; and placed upon precisely the same legal footing, in the same sentence ; the identical words, without even a repetition, covering them all—nor " shall deprive any person of life, liberty, or property without due process of law." No one has attempted to maintain the proposition, that a person can be lawfully deprived of his *life* or *liberty* without an opportunity to be heard, nor has any one, so far as I am aware, endeavored to show that " due process of law," as ·a general rule, respecting notice, and an opportunity to be heard, means one thing with reference to depriving one of life and liberty, and something else, with reference to depriving him of property. Counsel only seek to maintain that " due process of law " does not, *universally*, require an opportunity to be heard, as a condition of lawfully depriving one of his property, without considering the other branch of the proposition. It devolves upon those who maintain that there is a difference in the signification of this clause, as a general rule, when applied to life and liberty and when applied to property, to clearly establish it; and if there is an exception to the universality of the rule, to point it out, and show that the case under consideration is within the exception.

In combating the principle stated it is insisted that the language used by the court is too broad; that there are cases—peculiar cases—as shown by the authority cited, to which it is inapplicable. If this were so, it would only appear that there may be exceptions to the general rule, depending upon special circumstances and long established usage. It would then be necessary to show that the case in hand is within some recognized exception, and this has not been done.

In the *San Mateo Case* we disclaimed any attempt to give an accurate definition of the term " due process of law," which should be " applicable to all cases," as it was not deemed " necessary for the determination of that case." This disclaimer left room for exceptions founded upon long recognized and well-established usage. We there said that " to take one's property by taxation is to deprive one of his property; *and if not taken in pursuance of the law of the land,* in some due and recognized course of proceedings *based upon well recognized principles in force before and at the time this clause was first introduced into the various constitutions and the legislation of the country*— is to take it without due process of law." The doctrine was recognized that those forms and courses of proceeding based upon well-recognized principles in force before and at the time of the adoption of our National Constitution, would be " due process of law." The case of *Murray's Lessee et al.* vs. *Hoboken Land and Improvement Company,* (18 How., 274,) is a case of the kind—an exception to the ordinary rule of law depending upon the peculiar character, conditions, and circumstances of the case.

The mode of proceeding in this particular class of cases had the sanction of long-established usage in England before and down to the settlement of our country; and Mr. Justice Curtis' whole opinion is a labored effort to show, that the case he was discussing, was an exception to the ordinary rule of law, dependent alone upon long-established and exceptional usage. The case was that of a *defaulting public officer,* who had collected a large amount of public revenue of the United States, and appropriated it to his own use. The act of Congress provided a summary mode of proceeding to collect the money from him. It provided, among other things, for an auditing of the defaulting official's accounts, and certifying the amount due by the proper officers of the Treasury (the accounts are made up from the returns of the officer himself, and are *matters of record* in the Treasury Department); that when so audited and certified, it should become a lien on the property of the defaulting officer, which should be enforced by seizure and sale, under a distress warrant, issued by the solicitors of the Treasury. The Constitution having invested the judicial power in the courts, and declared that the judicial power shall extend to controversies to which the United States are a party, the questions were, whether these acts, under the statute of 1820, were an exercise of judicial power, vested solely in the courts; and if not an exercise of judicial power, whether such a seizure, under the warrant, without the action of the judicial power, did not deprive the party of his property " without due process of law," in violation of the provisions of the Constitution on that point. Or, as stated by Mr. Justice Curtis himself,

the questions were, whether " a collector of customs, from
whom a balance of account has been found to be due by
accounting officers of the Treasury, designated for that
purpose by law, can be deprived of his liberty, or property,
in order to enforce payment of that balance, without the
exercise of the judicial power of the United States, and
yet by 'due process of law,' within the meaning of those
terms in the Constitution; and if so, then, secondly,
whether the warrant in question was such due process of
law ?" He discusses the question as to what is meant by
"due process of law," and concludes, that a distress warrant, so far as the warrant itself is concerned, is due process of law, provided there is no judicial action necessary as a basis for it; for Congress can prescribe any
kind of process, so far as the form and mode of issue
is concerned. He then discusses the question, as to
whether the action of the Treasury Department, in auditing and certifying the account, constituted a sufficient
basis for the warrant to make the proceeding due process
of law. There being nothing in the Constitution to expressly authorize the proceeding, he " looked to the usages
and modes of proceedings existing in the common and
statute laws of England, before the emigration of our an-
cestors from England, and which are not shown to have
been unsuited to their civil and political condition by having been acted on by them after the settlement of this
country." He found in regard to debtors of the King—
defaulting receivers of the revenue in particular—that a
summary remedy existed, and a writ of extent might be
levied upon their goods and lands; but " to authorize a
writ of extent, however, the debt must be *matter of record*
in the King's Exchequer." Thus the debt, was already
ascertained by matter of record.

" In regard to debts due upon simple contracts other
than those due from collectors of the revenue, and other
accountants of the Crown, the practice from very ancient
times has been to issue a commission to inquire as to the

nature of the debt"—a proceeding of a strictly judicial nature and, therefore, due process of law. These proceedings were had under various acts of Parliament—that omnipotent legislative body which could repeal *Magna Charta* itself.

Justice Curtis proceeds: " This brief sketch of the modes of proceeding to ascertain and enforce payment of balances due from receivers of the revenue in England, is sufficient to show that the methods of ascertaining the existence and amount of *such* debts, and compelling their payment, *have varied widely* from the *usual* course of the common law *on other subjects;* and that as respects *such* debts, due from *such* officers, the law of the land, authorized the employment of auditors, and an inquisition without notice, and a species of execution, bearing a very close resemblance to what is termed a warrant of distress in the act of 1820, now in question." " It is certain, that this *diversity* in the law of the land, between *public defaulters* and *ordinary debtors*, was understood in this country and entered into the legislation of the colonies and provinces, and more especially of the States, after the Declaration of Independence, and before the formation of the Constitution of the United States."

As thus seen, this mode of enforcing the payment of balances was limited to defaulting collectors, and " receivers of the public revenues of England, and where the debts *were of record* in the King's Exchequer." And it shows that the methods of ascertaining the existence and amount of *such* debts and compelling their payment have *varied widely from the usual course of the common law on other subjects;* " and as respects *such* debts due from *such* officers, ' the law of the land ' authorized " a summary process similar to that of the law of 1820; and " this diversity in the ' law of the land ' between public defaulters and ordinary debtors was understood in this country." Thus, this mode of proceeding was an exception to the general rule as to what is " the law of the land," or " due process of law," made in favor of the King against those who accepted office from him, under and subject to laws burdened, at the time, with peculiar and stringent remedies, and then violated their duties and trusts by appropriating the public revenues collected, instead of putting them into the Treasury; and whose indebtedness was "matter of record in the King's Exchequer." This exception is recognized by the Court, but *as an exception*, and the decision is put upon the ground that it *is an exception*, and not the rule. "For," says Mr. Justice Curtis, "though 'due process of law' *generally* implies actor, reus, judex, regular allegations, *opportunity to answer, and a trial according to some settled course of judicial proceedings* (2 Inst., 47, 50; *Hoke* vs. *Henderson*, 4 Dev., N. C., 15; *Taylor* vs. *Porter*, 4 Hill, 146; *Van Zant* vs. *Waddell*, 2 Yerg., 260; *State Bank* vs. *Cooper*, id., 599; *Jones' Heirs* vs. *Perry*, 10 id., 59; *Green* vs. *Briggs*, 1 Curtis, 311), yet this is not *universally* true." An *exception*, then, is found in cases against *defaulting public officers whose debts are of record*. And such was the case of *Murray's Lessee* vs. *Hoboken Land and Improvement Company*.

The Court, in speaking of duties levied, and of defaulting officers, further says: "What officers should be appointed to collect the revenue thus authorized to be raised, and to disburse it in payment of the debts of the United States; what duties should be required of them; when and how, and to whom they should account, and what security they should furnish, and to *what remedies they should be subjected to enforce the proper discharge of their duties, Congress was to determine.* In the exercise of their powers, they have required collectors of customs to be appointed; made it incumbent on them to account, from time to time, with certain officers of the Treasury Department, and to furnish sureties by bond for the payment of all balances of the public money which may become due from them. And by the act of 1820, now in question, they have undertaken to provide *summary means to compel these officers—and in case of their default, their sureties—to pay such balances of the public money as may* be in their hands."

Whatever may have been the grounds of the distinction originally made between defaulters of the public revenue and other citizens, the case of such defaulting officers is clearly shown to be an exception to the general rule, resting upon very special circumstances, and the case cited and relied on *is a striking illustration of the maxim that " the exception proves the rule."*

But, again, under the statute of 1820, (3 Stat. U. S., 595,) by the provisions of section 4, the party did in fact have an opportunity to be heard before he could be deprived of his property. That section provided "that if any person should consider himself aggrieved by any warrant issued under this act, he may prefer a bill of complaint to any District Judge of the United States, setting forth the nature and extent of the injury of which he complains," and have a hearing. It is true that there was a determination of his liability, and process issued, which would become final and conclusive if he did not ask for a hearing, and Mr. Justice Curtis observes upon this section: " The act of 1820 makes such a provision for reviewing the decision of the accounting officers of the Treasury. But until it is reviewed it is final and binding." So in all cases of taxes under the Constitution of California, except where the assessment is by the State Board of Equalization, the assessment is first made by the assessor, and the tax-payer may afterwards, on a proper petition, have the action of the assessor reviewed by the Board of Equalization, and thus have an opportunity to be heard before his property is finally appropriated; yet, if he does not apply for such review, the tax levy becomes final and conclusive, and will be collected in the ordinary way by seizure and sale, or such other means as may be provided.

Both the ordinary tax-payer under the laws of California and the defaulting officers under the act of 1820, therefore, have an opportunity to be heard before their property can be finally appropriated, in a similar sense, and at a corresponding stage of the proceeding. If the opportunity thus afforded the tax-payer is in accordance with due process of law within the general rule, it is not apparent why the opportunity afforded the defaulting officer by the act of 1820 is not also. They both stand upon the same footing as to the time when an opportunity to be heard is given—the first determination before a hearing being only provisional; the accounting and seizure under the act of 1820 being something in the nature of an attachment to secure a lien, with an opportunity to be afterwards heard if the amount claimed by the Government is not, in fact, due.

In our judgment, this case in no sense or particular conflicts with the point decided by us as to the general rule—and the rule applicable to that case—in the *San Mateo County Case;* on the contrary, we think it a strong case to support the rule. It was cited by counsel and considered by us in the *San Mateo Case,* but we did not think it militated against our decision, and we did not deem it necessary to extend the discussion by noticing it in the opinions delivered. But after carefully reviewing the case, in consequence of its being so confidently relied on, and the only one relied on, as being inconsistent with our decision on this point, we think it may well be cited by us as a strong authority in support of our judgment. These tax cases certainly are not within the exception recognized in that case. The case is the only authority cited—unless the *Illinois Railroad Tax Cases* (92 U. S., 575) were so regarded by counsel—claimed to be in conflict with our decision on this point, and the Hoboken Land Case cited had no relation at all to what is necessary to constitute a valid levy of a public tax. No authority was cited to show that a tax levy upon property to be assessed upon evidence of its value is one of the exceptions to the general rule, that an opportunity to be heard before property can be taken from its owner and appropriated to public use, is an essential element of "due process of law."

In the Illinois Railroad Tax Cases, referred to by counsel, the points discussed and relied on were, that the act under which the tax was levied and equalized was void as being in contravention of the Constitution of Illinois; and that the bills in chancery filed presented no case for an injunction, for the reason that there had been no payment or tender of so much of the tax as was conceded ought to be paid. The court rested its decision mainly upon the latter ground, but also held that as the Supreme Court of Illinois, had decided the act not to be in contravention of the State Constitution, that decision would control the action of the Courts of the United States. The Court, however, expressed its concurrence with the views of the State Supreme Court on that point. In the course of the opinion delivered, it was said, that the State Board of Equalization of Illinois, in equalizing the taxes of the several counties—the equalization being by classes and counties—need give no notice to individual tax-payers, other than such as the law afforded; but, as I understand the decision, this was said with reference to the point, whether the statute was valid under the State Constitution. There does not appear to have been any point argued, or relied on, as to what constitutes "due process of law;" and the court in its decision does not decide, discuss, or even allude to the question, as to what are the necessary elements of "due process of law," with reference to taxation, or otherwise, within the meaning of the Fourteenth Amendment to the National Constitution. That question was, evidently, not considered. We, therefore, do not regard the observations made in the course of the opinion upon statutory notice in its relation to the equalization of taxes, on the question of the validity of the statute under the State Constitution, or other casual remarks upon points not argued, or well considered, as authoritative upon the point now under consideration.

This case, as was the *San Mateo Case*, has been laboriously prepared, and elaborately argued by many eminent counsel, and if the industry of the Attorney-General, and of a large number of attorneys and special counsel for the numerous counties interested has failed to find any recognition of the principle they were endeavoring to maintain, either in the practice of the several States, in the text-books, or decisions, or even *dicta* of the courts, we think it will be safe to presume that none can be found. The assertion of counsel, which is extraordinary for the positiveness with which it is made, that the court "finds no warrant whatever in the books" for the views expressed in the *San Mateo Case*, that an opportunity to be heard, before property can be compulsorily taken from a person in the form of a general tax upon property, is an essential element in " due process of law," may be attributed to the zeal of the advocate. It is not founded upon any pretense that the language quoted from the various cases cited, is not found in the decisions, but on the ground that in some of the cases the decision did not turn upon the precise point, whether such an opportunity is an essential element of " due process of law," and that in other cases the question arose in relation to local assessments for street improvements and the like, and not on assessments for taxes for general revenue under laws providing for the ordinary general expenses of the State, county, or city.

As to the first class of cases, one of the counsel of the defendants well says, and his language is adopted as a clear general statement of a principle often acted upon by the courts: "The existence of doctrines and rules of law is often shown and established by a continuous and uniform series of judicial *dicta*, incorporated into their opinions by judges *arguendo*, although, perhaps, the actual facts of the cases under discussion did not absolutely require the statement of such doctrines or rules. And here you will discriminuate. . . . . These expressions of judicial opinion may be correct, or may not be correct. They may be expressions of well-settled rules, of well-settled and established principles—principles, the statement of which is not absolutely necessary to the final decision—and yet a continuous and uniform series of such judicial statements is often very high, in fact the highest evidence of the existence of the rule of law which they do set out. One simple *dictum* may not be of much weight, or it might have much weight, depending largely upon the ability, the character, and authority of the judge. But a uniform *concensus* of such judicial expressions of opinion, even when they are *dicta* of different judges in various courts, especially when they have been accepted by able text-writers, and not contradicted by a single direct decision, is as high evidence of a doctrine or rule as can be found."

In all the cases of this class cited by the court, even if the decision did not turn upon this point of constitutional law, the discussion was cognate to it, and the Judges clearly and distinctly stated the right to an opportunity to be heard, as a *constitutional* right. Some of these declarations can scarcely be called *dicta*, and they relate both to general taxation and local assessments. While such assertions of the principle of law may not be of so controlling a character as a decision of a court of acknowledged authority, directly determining the point in issue upon mature consideration, they are, certainly, of some authority, as being the deliberately expressed opinions of eminent Judges, and entitled to great weight. So, also, so distinguished a jurist and text-writer as Chief Justice Cooley, gives it as his deliberate opinion—as well as states it as a rule drawn from the authorities cited by him—that notice of the proceedings and opportunity to be heard are essential. His language is: " We should say that notice of proceedings in such cases and an opportunity for a hearing of some description were matters of constitutional right. It has been customary to provide for them, as a part of what is ' due process of law ' for these cases, and it is not to be assumed that constitutional provisions, carefully framed for the protection of property, were intended, or could be construed to sanction legislation under which officers might secretely assess one for any amount in their discretion, without giving him an opportunity to contest the justice of the assessment. It has often been pointedly and emphatically declared that it is contrary to the first principles of justice that one should be condemned unheard; and it has also been justly observed of taxing officers that 'it would be a dangerous precedent to hold that any absolute power resides in them to tax, as they may choose, without giving any notice to the owner. It is a power liable to great abuse,' and it might safely have been added, it is a power that under such circumstances would be certain to be abused." "The general principles of law applicable to such tribunals oppose the exercise of any such power."

In the other class of cases arising out of local assessments the point was directly in issue, and the point in the case upon which the decision turned, and in no case was there any distinction drawn between taxation for special local purposes and general taxation. There can be no difference. In either case, whether general taxation or local assessment for special purposes, the tax or assessment is levied and collected under and by virtue of the sovereign power of taxation. There is no difference in the power or principle exercised. The only difference recognized is the difference in the mode of ascertaining the proper amount to be paid by each. Both are assessed and collected for a public purpose, as the party's share of the public burden, but the local assessment is distributed over a smaller number of persons and a more limited territory, and is usually assessed upon that part of the property supposed to be especially benefited. It is not always, and perhaps not usually, assessed according to the value of the property, but according to benefits, or according to the square foot or front foot or number of acres, or on some such principle or of apportionment. It is as necessary to apportion it according to some fixed, uniform rule, requiring action of a judicial nature, as in the case of general taxa-

tion. This rule is the only distinction recognized—both
systems of assessment and collection resting ultimately
upon the sovereign power of taxation. *Emory vs. The
City of San Francisco*, 28 Cal., 349, and *People vs. Mayor
of Brooklyn*, 4 Com., 420, well illustrate the only distinction between general taxation and local assessments, and
none affect the point under discussion. In both it is necessary to ascertain the amount, extent, and character of
the property which forms the basis of the public charge,
and on account of which it is to be collected; in order to
properly apportion to each owner his proper share of the
public burden. There is as great necessity for him to
have an opportunity to be heard before the tax, in the case
of general taxation becomes final, as there is in the case
of an assessment for local purposes, as street improvements. The levying and collection of taxes for general purposes, under laws providing for general taxation, are just
as clearly a depriving of the owner of his property as the
levy and collection of a street or other assessment for local
purposes. It is impossible to distinguish them on this
point, and no distinction is made in the books. A decision of the point, as to notice and opportunity to be heard
in a case of a street assessment, is just as clearly an authority directly in point on the question at issue as though
made in a case of general taxation, and it would be equally
controlling. The authorities arising upon the assessment
cited, therefore, are, in our judgment, authorities directly
and fully in point.

Again, so far as we are advised—and such is the statement in the books, which has not been controverted—it
has been the usual practice in the legislation of all the
States, at some point in the proceedings, to levy and collect a tax based upon property, where it is necessary to
ascertain its amount, character, and value, before the liability becomes finally and irrevocably fixed, to give to the
owner or tax-payer an opportunity to be heard. Such has
always been, and is now, the case under the Constitution

6

of California, except as to railroads operated in more than one county; and where there has been a departure from the rule, and the validity of such statutes litigated, on the ground of want of due process of law, as we have seen, the statutes have been overthrown. The fact of such general practice in legislation is very persuasive evidence that, in the estimation of the legislators and people of the several states, an opportunity to be heard in such cases is an important element in " due process of law." This is of itself authority entitled to serious consideration. As the case stands, then, no decision of any Court, no *dictum* of any respectable judge, other than so far as the cases cited may be so regarded, no passage from any text-writer has been brought to our notice which is in direct conflict with the law and principles as stated in the citations made by us on this point in the *San Mateo Case.*

In view of the numerous *dicta*—conceding them to be, properly, *dicta*—of able judges in one class of cases cited; of the able decisions, directly in point, in the other class arising under local assessment laws; of the assumption of the existence of the rule by the United States Supreme Court in *Davidson* vs. *New Orleans;* of the adoption and laying down of the rule by text-writers of the highest eminence and judicially recognized authority; in view of the general legislation of the States upon the subject, from the beginning recognizing, and, practically, acting upon the principle, and in view of the further fact, that no decision of a judge, or statement of the rule by text-writers to the contrary, has been brought to our notice, we think that the Court was fully justified, in the *San Mateo Case,* in expressing the belief, that the authorities established beyond all controversy, that somewhere in the proceeding of assessing a tax upon property, where it is necessary to ascertain its amount, character, and value, as a means of apportionment under a law, or State Constitution—at some point before the amount of the assessment becomes finally and irrevocably fixed—the statute, or State Constitution, must provide for notice to be given to the owner of the property taxed, and an opportunity be afforded to make objections and be heard upon them. *If this defendant, on its large amount of property, can be lawfully taxed unheard, then it is competent for the State to abolish all right to be heard, and every person can be taxed unheard at the arbitrary will of the taxing officers.*

We have never contended that some species of taxes, as a poll tax, license tax upon occupations, trades, etc., where the tax is specific, and not *ad valorem*, and does not depend upon the amount of the business done, and the like, may not be levied without an opportunity to be heard. Taxes of these and like kinds operate upon all alike, and a hearing would be of no possible avail. The law itself fixes the amount. It is a legislative act, wherein the objects of taxation are indicated, and amount fixed alike for all, leaving nothing of a judicial nature to inquire into or determine. But, where the tax is based upon the amount, character, condition, and value of property, the amount of business, income, etc., and it is necessary to inquire into, examine, hear evidence, and decide upon these matters, in order to assign to each individual his proper share of the public burden, he is entitled to notice of some kind, and an opportunity to be heard, before the extent of his liability is finally and irrevocably fixed. The notice may not be required to be personal to each individual, or anything other than statutory, but the statute should fix some time within, and place at which, he may appear, and must give to the tax-payer a right and some opportunity to appear and be heard upon the matter. He may not succeed in reducing his tax, but the law affording an opportunity presumes that justice will be done upon proper hearing and proofs, by the officers charged with the duty of doing justice in these matters. To the suggestion that a party is as much entitled to be heard upon the fixing of the rate of taxation, as to ascertaining the kind, amount, and value of the property, it is sufficient to observe that fixing the rate is a matter of legislative discretion and a legislative act. An estimate of the amount óf revenue required—the probable total amount of property upon which it must be imposed being made—the rate is fixed by the Legislature upon that basis, making the allowance, suggested by experience, for inability to collect the whole tax. When fixed, it operates equally upon all. It is only when it is necessary to ascertain the kind, amount, condition, and value of each man's property for the purpose of apportioning his proper share of the burden, that it is necessary to act judicially, and to give an opportunity to be heard before the amount shall be finally and irrevocably fixed.

Second. We are of the opinion, expressed in the *San Mateo Case,* that the statement required by section 3,664 of the Political Code, as adopted in 1880, does not afford notice and an opportunity to be heard sufficient to constitute " due process of law," within the meaning of the constitutional provision, for the reasons there stated. (8 Sawyer, 296.) In this case, the assessment was, *largely,* in excess of the valuation furnished by the railroad officials, in pursuance of section 3,664. As to the supposed Statutes of 1881, an error in the *printed* journal appears, which was not called to our attention at the hearing of the San Mateo case. Upon counting the names of those appearing among the ayes in the printed journal (Jour. Ass., 24th session, page 472) there are found to be forty-one names, which constitute just a majority, although they are footed up as thirty-nine, and the announcement by the Speaker was, that there were thirty-nine ayes, and thirty-two noes. The Speaker declared " that this was not the final action on the bill, and that the House had concurred in Senate amendments to Assembly Bill No. 475, by a vote of thirty-nine ayes, to thirty-two noes." (Id., 473.) Mr. Paulk appealed from the decision of the Chair, " on the ground that forty-one votes were required for concurrence." On motion of Mr. Hoitt, this appeal *was laid on the table.* Mr. Hale filed a protest, the ground being " that on vote taken on the motion to concur in the said Senate amendments, and *the only action* taken by this Assembly on said bill, as amended in the Senate, whereby it was passed by the Assembly, there was less than a majority of the members of the Assembly voting therefor; and, therefore, said bill, having upon such final vote received less than a constitutional majority of the Assembly, I protest, as aforesaid, that said bill should have been declared lost." (Id., 475.) The Speaker then again " stated that the action on Senate amendments to the bill *was not a final action on the bill,* and, consequently, concurrence or non-concurrence in the amendments required a majority vote only." (Id., 475.) Mr. Griffith thereupon said: " The decision of the Speaker and the House, to the effect that less than a majority of the whole can concur in an amendment which may take all the virtue out of a bill, I regard as dangerous. . . . . Wherefore I desire to enter my solemn protest against such proceedings." (Id., 475.) And Mr. Kellogg said: " I desire to have my protest entered upon the journal of this Assembly against the decision of the Speaker, in declaring that the Assembly had concurred in the Senate amendments to the bill, . . . for the reason that the journal shows that forty-one members did not vote aye in concurring with said amendments."

This was the last action of the House on this bill. It will be seen, then, that, while upon counting up the ayes in the *printed* journal forty-one names are found, yet that they were footed up and carried out as thirty-nine; the vote was announced by the Speaker as thirty-nine, and the whole subsequent action of the House was upon the assumption that there were but thirty-nine. Upon comparing the *printed* journal with the *original written* journal, however, on file in the office of the Secretary of State, it is conceded, on all sides, that they do not agree in the names voting aye, the original *written* journal containing only forty names, one of the names in the *printed* journal *not appearing in the written* journal. We are of opinion that the written journal is the authentic official record, and that it corresponds with, and is sustained by, all the other parts of the printed journal, and with the announcement of the Speaker, and all the action of the House, and that it must control. It, therefore, affirmatively appears that the act never passed, and never became a law of the State of California.

Besides, it was officially announced by the Speaker at the time, and so recorded, that this *was not the final passage of the bill*, and that it was on this ground that the amendments were concurred in by a vote less than the number required by the Constitution on the *final* passage of a bill. There was no appeal from this decision, and it does not appear to have been revoked. No other vote appears to have been had, or other announcement by the Speaker made in regard to this bill. No other action was had by the House, except on March 4th, being the last act before adjournment *sine die*, the bill was reported as correctly enrolled, and as having been presented to the Governor for approval. No action was taken on this report, and the bill does not appear to have been reported to the House as having been approved. At the time of the adjournment of the Legislature, therefore, there was an appeal pending, lying on the table, liable to be called up at any time from the very decision of the Chair declaring the amendments to be concurred in. Thus, there had been no final action on this question, unless the report of the Committee on Enrollment, without further action thereon, can be so regarded, and the whole matter was still in the control of the House, and unfinished business, when the Legislature was dissolved by adjournment and lapse of time.

At the time the assessment in question was made, then, neither the Constitution nor any statute of California gave the defendant any right, or afforded it any legal notice of the proceeding, or opportunity to be heard as to the correctness or propriety of the assessment. The assessment was an arbitrary exercise of power by the State Board of Equalization, according to its own will and pleasure. It is true that in some of the cases, *though not in this case,* an agent of defendant did appear before the board, after the assessment was made, and sought to get the assessment reduced; and the board, after hearing the application, refused to reduce the assessment, but upon what grounds it does not appear. The defendant offered to show, by the testimony of members of the board, upon what ground the refusal was made, but the evidence was ruled out on the objection of the plaintiff that it was incompetent. As there was no law authorizing such an application or hearing, or authorizing a modification of the assessment by the board upon such application, and the listening to the application was a mere matter of grace, it is the legal presumption that the board acted in conformity with the law and put its refusal on that ground—that it would be unlawful to reduce the amount. But whether it did or not can make no difference.

If such a right and opportunity to be heard is an essential element of " due process of law," the law must provide for it as a right. The party is not required to accept the boon by the favor or good nature of the officers. And as the proceeding would be wholly without the pale of the law, it will not be presumed that the board would act with that nice regard to judicial fairness, or that proper sense of judicial responsibility, that would characterize their proceedings when acting wholly within the limits of their official duties as imposed upon them by law.

Third. The next question is whether the provision of the State Constitution, under which the assessment in question was made, is in conflict with the clause of the Fourteenth Amendment to the National Constitution, which provides that no state " shall deny to any person within its jurisdiction the equal protection of the laws." In order that my views on this point may be presented in a connected, unbroken order, I shall adopt the reasoning contained in the discussion of the fifth point of my opinion in the *San Mateo Case*, with such additional observations, incorporated at the proper places, as occur to me, illustrative of the views entertained. In the forcible and accurate language of Mr. Edmunds, which I cannot improve, the "Fourteenth Amendment was a new *Magna Charta* that was in fact, in form, and in effect a fundamental security to every person in the state in respect of every private right that could be invaded; and an absolute affirmation of equality of civil rights to all persons before the law. The first clause forbids the state to touch life, liberty, or property without due process of law; and the second forbids that *even with* due process of law any person shall be denied the equal protection of the laws. This is the plain letter of the amendment. It is its intrinsic and beneficent spirit, and it was its purpose." . . . .

"What, then, is equality of protection? A *civil* right *under* a government is a distinct thing from a *political* right *in* it; thus a state may deny to females the right to vote, but it cannot deny to them the right to sue in courts or impose on their property all the burdens of the community. To hold otherwise would lead to the affirmation of the right of the State to make race, or color, or religion, or age, or stature the criterion of *civil* rights, and to exert the absolute right of confiscation by classes or descriptions; for, in such a case, every person of that class or description would stand on an equality with his fellow-victims."

"It is not denied that a State may classify the persons who are to perform certain public duties or bear certain public burdens, based upon personal peculiarities of either sex or calling, etc., as to require military service only from males, or to exempt females from a poll tax, and impose license tax upon certain trades, or tax all franchises of corporations and their special privileges; but it could not impose a poll tax on one-half its male or female citizens that it did not impose on the rest *in like degree*. And when we come to the case of property, *as property*, to be affected by a tax, or any other imposition imposed upon it as a *thing* of *value*, a distinction cannot be made to depend upon character, or occupation, or quality, or any individual characteristic of the citizen. To hold otherwise would be to set up the very essence of tyranny and arbitrary power."

" '*Equal* protection' is the *same* protection under the *same* circumstances; all are to stand alike in like intrinsic conditions. Holding property *as property* is certainly a like intrinsic condition. In the administration of justice, if the criterion of a right to sue be value, all must have the same right when the same value is concerned; or if the criterion be the nature of the controversy, all must have the same right whose cases are of the same nature. This appears to be too clear for discussion."

" So, too, in the matter of taxation, if the tax, as in this case, be laid upon the *values* of property, all persons must stand on the same footing, according to the value of their respective property, as to the proportionate burden they are to bear in respect to the value."

" The farmer must be assessed at the same rate for the value of his land as the lawyer for the value of his land, and he must have the same right of notice and hearing, etc., as his fellow citizens of other callings; and if deductions are provided to be made from values on account of debts (which is only a method of reaching effective value) of one class of citizens, they must be made from those of other classes, without reference to what particular characteristics as citizens or persons they may have, as sex, or race, or age, or quality, or calling."

" The *basis* of the imposition being *property, as such,* the fact that certain property is owned by a corporation, or a white man, or man of bad character, or a clergyman, cannot be made the ground of a levy, that, both in form, in fact, and in result, is unequal and injurious. Any other doctrine necessarily implies that the State may carry such unequal exactions to the end of complete confiscation by edict of all the property of any class, or man, who, during the passion of the hour, may not be in the sunshine of popularity."

It is insisted that the constitutional provision under which the tax in question is levied does not deny to the defendant the equal protection of the laws, and it is sought to maintain the validity of the provision on the ground that it is a proper exercise of the principle of classification—that the property is classified according to its condition and use—and on that ground properly taxed upon a basis different from that applied to other property. The provision to be considered is as follows:

"A mortgage, deed of trust, contract, or other obligation by which a debt is secured, shall, for the purposes of assessment and taxation, be deemed and treated as an interest in the property affected thereby. *Except as to railroad and other quasi public corporations,* in case of debts so secured, the value of the property affected by such mortgage, deed of trust, contract or obligation, less the value of such security, shall be assessed to the owner of the property, and the value of such security shall be assessed and taxed to the owner thereof, in the county, city, or district in which the property affected thereby is situate. The taxes so levied shall be a lien upon the property and security, and may be paid by either party to such security; if paid by the owner of such security, the tax so levied upon the property affected thereby shall become a part of the debt so secured; if the owner of the property shall pay the tax so levied on such security, it shall constitute a payment thereon, and to the extent of such payment a full discharge thereof: *Provided,* that if any such security or indebtedness shall be paid by any such debtor or debtors, after assessment and before the tax levy, the amount of such levy may likewise be retained by such debtor or debtors, and shall be computed according to the tax levy for the preceding year."

Whatever the property, then, real or personal, mortgaged to secure a debt, the value of the debt so secured, in the case of everybody, "*except a railroad and other quasi-public corporation*," is to be deducted from the value of the property mortgaged, and the value only of the property mortgaged, "less the value of such security, shall be assessed and taxed to the owner of the property, and the value of such security shall be assessed and taxed to the owner thereof." That is to say, that the property is to be divided between the parties according to the value of their respective interests, and whatever the nature or extent of the interest of each in the property may be, it shall be taxed to the real owner. But in the case of "a railroad or other *quasi* public corporation," there is to be no reduction of the value of the mortgaged property—no division according to the interests of each—and the whole is to be taxed to one party, although he, in reality, does not *own* the whole. In one case, if property is mortgaged to the extent of half its value, the owner is taxed upon one-half the value, and the owner of the debt secured, or the mortgagee, is taxed upon the other half. But in the other case, the owner of the legal title to the property is assessed and taxed upon the whole value of the property, and the other party, who is interested to the extent of one-half, upon none. A, a natural person, or even a corporation other than one of the excepted class, has $50,000 in cash—all the property he has—and purchases of B, another natural person, a piece of real estate for $100,000, that being its actual value, paying one-half down, and giving a mortgage for $50,000 to secure the balance of the purchase-money. The Constitution in effect says—and in this instance such is the real substantial state of facts—that A and B each has $50,000 in the property, one-half not having been paid for by A, and each shall be assessed and pay a tax upon his own interest in it, amounting to $50,-000. A, in this instance, is worth only $50,000, and if he pays taxes upon a larger amount, he pays taxes upon property he does not really own—upon property owned by somebody else. This seems to be a self-evident proposition.

C, "a railroad, or other *quasi* public corporation," also has $50,000 cash, and purchases of B, for its proper use, an adjoining piece of real estate for $100,000, which is also its actual value, paying $50,000, and giving a mortgage to secure the balance of the purchase-money. In this case, as in the other, the actual interest of each in the property is $50,000. They stand precisely upon the same footing in all particulars with reference to the property. C has only $50,000 in the property—it not having paid for the other half—and B, the rest. But in this case the Constitution says that C shall, nevertheless, be assessed for and pay taxes upon the whole property, *double* the amount he *really owns, and B shall not be required to pay anything.* That is to say, that C shall not only pay the tax on its own property, but the tax upon B's property; that money, to the amount of the tax assessed upon $50,000, belonging to B, shall be taken by the State or county from C, and appropriated to the use and for the benefit of B, to liquidate B's share of the public burdens. This sum, being so much more than C's share of the public burdens, and being in fact B's share, *the result of the operation is, not only to take so much property from C, for public use, without compensation, but also to arbitrarily take it from C and apply it to the use and benefit of another private party, B, without compensation. The result would be the same, whether the property of A, B and C, thus situated and mortgaged, is land, a railroad operated in one or more counties, or any other kind of property.*

Does a law which authorizes such proceedings—such discriminations—bear or press equally upon A and C, or equally upon B and C? Is C equally protected in its rights of property with A, or equally protected with B, *or equally with all other natural persons,* or all corporations other than railroad or other *quasi* public corporations? Although situated precisely alike with reference to their property, do they feel the pressure of the public burdens equally and alike ? The question does not appear to me to admit of argument. Upon the very statement of the proposition, it seems to me to be self-evident that a law authorizing and *requiring* such proceedings does not afford, but expressly *denies*, the equal protection of the laws. The Constitution, in the one case, says that " the mortgage, deed of trust, contract, or obligation " shall be " deemed and treated as an interest in the land affected thereby," which, in the cases supposed, together with the debt secured, it undoubtedly, in fact, is; but, in effect, the Constitution says it is not so in the other case. Different kinds of property may require to be taxed in different forms and modes, in order to be equally taxed. And classifications of property for purposes of taxation should have reference to the just equality of burdens, so far as that is practically attainable. Classification should have reference to the different character, situation, and circumstances of the property, making a different form or mode of taxation proper, if not absolutely necessary. It cannot be arbitrarily made, with mere reference to the nationality, color, or character of the owners, whether natural or artificial persons, without any reference to a difference in the character, situation, or circumstances of the property. Should second mortgagees foreclose a mortgage on a railroad or other property of a " railroad or other *quasi* public corporation," and a natural person become the purchaser of the road or other property subject to the prior mortgage, at the next annual assessment the amount of the first mortgage bonds or indebtedness secured would be deducted from the value of the road or other property, and the amount of the bonds or other indebtedness assessed to the mortgagees. Such, also, would be the result in the case before supposed if C—a railroad or other *quasi* public corporation—should convey its land to a natural person, subject to the mortgage to B; and although there would be no change in the condition, circumstances, use, or value of the property—the change being only in the owner—C's grantee would only be required to pay one-half the amount of taxes which C had been compelled to pay, and B, who before paid nothing, would be required to pay the other half. Should the Southern Pacific Railroad and its lands pass into the hands of a natural person upon a foreclosure and sale, under a second mortgage, subject to the mortgage now on them, the value of this very security would be deducted from the value of the property at the next annual assessment. Thus, although the property would in all respects be the same, and similarly situated, and applied to the same uses—for natural persons as well as corporations may own and operate railroads—a mere change in the ownership would require and effect an entire change in the mode and basis of the assessment, and the amount of taxes levied on the owner. Nothing, it seems to me, could more clearly demonstrate the unsoundness of the proposition, that only an admissible classification of property for the purposes of taxation is involved in the different schemes provided for taxing the property of "railroad and other *quasi* public corporations," and the property of natural persons and of other corporations. Railroad and other *quasi* public corporations are not even put upon the same footing with other corporations, the latter being placed upon an equality with natural persons. A mere change of ownership under the provisions in question largely affects the amount of taxes paid by the owner upon the same property, without any change in the character, condition, value, use, or circumstances of the property itself. A provision that a black man shall pay double the amount of taxes paid by a white man on the same kind of property similarly situated and used, or upon the identical property, in consequence of a mere change of ownership from a white man to a black man, might with as good reason be sustained on the principle of classification invoked. The classification in this case is clearly by ownership, and not by condition or use.

That natural persons may own and operate a railroad in this State as well as corporations is manifest from the fact that this road is mortgaged under the authority of the laws of the State, and this of itself necessarily involves the power to sell and convey, in case the occasion arises, under a decree of foreclosure, to any party who is willing to pay the highest price for the road. It also appears as a fact in this case that a natural person purchased a railroad operated in more than one county, extending from Marysville, in the county of Yuba, to Oroville, in the county of Butte, under a decree foreclosing a mortgage, received his conveyance therefor, and that he has been operating it and been assessed, and has paid taxes upon it for more than two years past. So, also, numerous statutes of the States were introduced in evidence, granting the right to natural persons, not incorporated, to build and operate railroads. "An act to provide for the construction of a railroad from Mokelumne City to Woodbridge, in the county of San Joaquin," (Statutes 1862, page 97,) and an act authorizing the building of a railroad from the Embarcadero, on the bay of Petaluma, in Sonoma County, (id., 295,) are examples of numerous acts of a similar character found scattered through the volumes of the statutes from that time to the present. Thus private parties owning and operating railroads covered by mortgages, and situated in all respects precisely as railroad corporations are situated with respect to the same kind of property, would only be required to pay taxes upon the excess of the value of the road or other property over the value of the security, while the holder of the security would be assessed for and pay the taxes on the value of the security. The personal liability of each would only extend to the tax on his own interest, and, in many instances, the value of the security would equal the whole value of the property, thereby relieving the mortgagor of all taxes on the property. This is not classification, therefore, by its condition or use, for the purposes of taxation at all, but by ownership.

There is no difference in the rate imposed; it is taxed according to its value, like all other property; no more, and no less tax, in the aggregate, is levied. It is, therefore, taxed upon the same principle as other property; no more and no less revenue is raised by the classification. The State is not benefited. The burden is simply taken from the owner and thrown upon one who does not own the property taxed. It is not taxed to and made a personal charge upon the owner as other property is under like circumstances. This is the only difference, and that does not affect the principle of the taxation. Unless it is competent to class the property of Jones, whether land, or railroad, or other property, when mortgaged, as belonging to Smith, and compel Smith to pay the taxes as a personal charge or liability imposed upon him on the property of Jones, who is not to be taxed or charged upon the property at all, when the same thing is not done as to other property of like kind and similarly situated, then this provision of the State Constitution cannot be maintained on the principle of classification or any other. The interests of the mortgagor and mortgagee are not the same—not identical. The estate of one begins where the estate of the other ends. They both together, under that clause which makes the mortgage in all cases—as it does in terms—an interest in the land, for the purpose of taxation, make up the whole, so far as classification for the purpose of taxation is concerned.

Suppose the position of the parties, the mortgagor and mortgagee in this case, in regard to the imposition and payment of the tax had been reversed, and the Constitution had imposed the tax upon the whole as a personal charge upon, and compelled payment by, the mortgagee —the holder of the security—instead of upon the mortgagor, the mortgagor not being taxed at all, would such a provision have been valid upon the principle of classification, or any other? Would the mortgagee stand upon the same footing with other mortgagees ? I apprehend that such a provision would not stand for a moment, in the presence of the provision of the National Constitution assuring to all the equal protection of the laws. Such a provision would not operate, equally, upon the two parties interested in the property, nor upon the mortgagee thus taxed, and other parties in like circumstances, where the mortgagors, are natural persons, or other corporations, who are only compelled to pay taxes upon the interests in property which they actually own. If the holder of the security could not be taxed for the interest held by the owner of the railroad, land, or other property mortgaged, no sound reason is apparent for holding that the mortgagor can be taxed for the whole, and especially where, as in this particular instance, the value of the security is greater than the value of the estate of the other party. There cannot be one law for one person, and a different and more onerous law for another, similarly situated, and both enjoy the equal protection of the laws in the particulars wherein such laws differ.

Conceding the Fourteenth Amendment to apply to taxation, as it undoubtedly does, I think I hazard little in saying that no possible reasoning can justify such classification or discrimination under it. That classification, upon such principles, is arbitrary, tyrannical, and unjustifiable.

There can be no valid classification of property, under the *State Constitution*, for the purposes of taxation, based upon the uses to which it is applied, except so far as the use may give additional value to the property; and the principle under the *constitutional provision requiring all property to be taxed at its value*, would only authorize the increase, or modification of the assessment, by adding the increased value, so arising from the use. One owner may pasture his land; another raise wheat, cotton, or sugar-cane; another plant a vineyard for the production of wine, or an orange grove; another erect buildings upon his land,

7

and enjoy the rents arising thorefrom; and another devote his to the construction and operation of a railroad. If any of these uses give additional value to the land or other property, it must still be taxed at its actual value, be it greater or less. But under the constitutional provision *requiring all property to be taxed at its actual value*, it cannot be classified by its uses, *for the purpose of applying other principles of taxation than value as a basis ; or for the purpose of taxing it according to ownership, so as to make one class of owners, as such, pay more than another; or one class of owners pay the taxes that ought to be assessed against and paid by another class.* The State Constitution does not profess to classify upon the basis of the uses to which property is applied. It recognizes no such principle in terms or by implication. It says nothing about uses; but classifies, in terms, by ownership, and includes all of the property of the same owners in its class for non-deduction of the value of the security—land and other property held for sale as well as property used for operating railroads, or other corporate uses of *quasi* public corporations, without making any reference whatever to its uses. The only rule by which any property is authorized to be assessed, is according to its value. The Constitution arbitrarily provides, as to a particular class, that they shall pay the taxes upon the interest—according to the constitutional definition of property—in the property held by another class of owners who are allowed to escape taxation altogether, and in this particular the laws do not bear upon or protect the former equally with the latter. It provides that railroads and other *quasi* public corporations shall pay taxes upon property they do not own—shall pay other people's taxes. This discrimination against such corporations is not a taxation but a confiscation of their property, *not for the benefit of the public, for there are no more taxes collected in the aggregate, but for the benefit of other property owners, who thereby escape their share of the public burdens.* If the arbitrary discrimination and classification found in this case can be legally made under the National Constitution and the law of the land, then the subordinate State Constitution or law can be so framed as to dispose of a man's rights in property of all kinds by arbitrary classification and definition, without regard to the real facts, circumstances, or condition of the property. A person may, by such subordinate statutory provisions, be classified and defined out of the equal protection of the laws guaranteed by the National Constitution; and if so with reference to this provision, he can also be classified and defined out of uniformity in the operation of the laws in other particulars; out of the protection of due process of law and of the provision forbidding a law impairing the obligation of contracts or taking property for public use without just compensation; and, indeed, out of all the guaranties of the Constitution, State or national. I am not arguing that property of all kinds may not be taxed where it is found, provided all owners are put upon the same footing; but in this case there is a personal liability sought to be enforced against the defendant for taxes not imposed upon others in like circumstances, without any means provided for reimbursement, such as are applicable to others similarly situated, by the party who ought to pay the tax.

For authorities, including decisions of the United States Supreme Court, illustrating this point, reference is made to the *San Mateo Case*, 8 Saw., 302-4.

It is argued that the taxing of the whole value of mortgaged property of railroads and other *quasi* public corporations to the corporation owning it, subject to the mortgage, while the same thing is not done with respect to the property of natural persons or other corporations similarly situated, is valid as being simply a *franchise* tax—a tax for the privilege of being a corporation, "a tax imposed as a return for privileges and powers not possessed by individuals." It is further said that it is not material by what standard a franchise tax is measured—whether the tax is in gross or measured by receipts, the amount of property acquired, or by any other standard; and cases are cited from some of the States where a franchise tax is claimed to have been sustained on such principles. But this view wholly ignores the provisions of the State Constitution itself on the subject. This is not, and does not purport to be, in any sense, a *franchise* tax: A *franchise* tax is otherwise in express terms provided for. The Constitution itself prescribes how a franchise tax shall be assessed; and that is, like all other property, "in proportion to its value." "All property . . . . shall be taxed in *proportion to its value, to be ascertained as provided by law*." (Art. XIII., sec. 1.) "The word property, as used in this article and section, is hereby declared to include money, credits, ... *franchises*, and all other matters and things . . . . capable of private ownership." (Ib.)

Again, "the *franchise*, roadway, etc., of all railroads operated in more than one county in this State shall be assessed by the State Board of Equalization *at their actual value*." (Ib., sec. 10.) Thus the *franchises* of the defendant, under the Constitution of California, can only be assessed like other property, according to "their actual value," be that more or less. Their *franchises* have, therefore, already been otherwise assessed at their value—all the Constitution will allow—and this discrimination is not, and cannot be, under the Constitution of California, a franchise tax. It has no reference to the franchise. It is simply in law, what it is in fact, an arbitrary and unjustifiable discrimination against railroad and other *quasi* public corporations, that cannot be maintained under the Fourteenth Amendment to the National Constitution, guaranteeing to every person the equal protection of the laws.

Great stress was laid in the arguments of plaintiffs' counsel upon the growing and overweening power and greed of corporations; and it was vehemently asserted that this is a struggle between the people and the corporations for supremacy; that corporations, by corrupt means, and through their large and widespread influence, have obtained, and they are obtaining, control of Legislatures, etc., etc.

If this be so, then it is of the utmost importance to every natural person in the United States that these guaranties of the Fourteenth Amendment to the National Constitution should be maintained in all their length and breadth. They are the only means of protection left to the people. If these unequal taxes can be imposed upon the class of corporations named in the Constitution, the position of the parties can be reversed, and the unequal tax now thrown upon the corporations may hereafter be imposed upon the other parties. If these can be taxed without a hearing, then all or any class of persons can be taxed without a hearing ; and if there is good ground for the alarm manifested by the counsel of the plaintiff, such corporations, when they acquire the deprecated power and control indicated, will not be likely to be slow in shifting the unequal burden to the other side. There is, therefore, upon that hypothesis, no safety to the people, except in most rigidly maintaining the guaranties of the Fourteenth Amendment in their broadest scope.

Fourth. Upon the point as to whether the provision of the State Constitution under which the tax in question was levied, is valid by virtue of the power of the State over corporations, under the authority reserved to the State under the Constitution to amend, alter, or repeal the laws under which they were organized, or otherwise, I refer to the quite full discussion of the point under the sixth head in my opinion in the *San Mateo Case*, 8 Saw., 304. I shall, however, make some additional observations.

In order to sustain the validity of the tax on that ground, the constitutional provision must operate as an amendment to the *general* statute of California, by which it imposes upon railroad and other *quasi* public corporations, under the amended statute, as a condition of their continued existence, a liability to be taxed otherwise than as natural persons and other corporations are taxed. It is not pretended by anybody that any express intention to

amend the act relating to corporations is found in the new
Constitution, or that any reference is anywhere made to
the act. The operation of the amendment of the statute
is sought to be worked out by implications, and the necessities of the case, which require the tax to be sustained on
that ground, as there is no other on which it can rest.
But repeals or amendments of statutes by implication
never were favored; and, under our Constitution, limiting
the power of the legislature to the passage of acts embrac-
ing but a single subject, which must be expressed in the
title of the act, and forbidding an amendment otherwise
than by re-enacting the whole section as amended, would
seem to render the rule still more restrictive in its operation. No reference to this matter of taxation is made in
any part of the chapter devoted to corporations. The
provision is found in the chapter providing for taxation, and
which deals with taxation, and *only taxation, as taxation.*
It is manifest, that the idea of amending the act relating
to corporations was never contemplated by the convention
in framing, or the people in adopting, the Constitution.
We are satisfied that the charge must be sustained, if
sustained at all, only as a tax, without reference to the
power of the State to impose further conditions upon
corporations not imposed at their creation by amendment to the general laws under which they became incorporated.

But if the State, under its power to amend the laws under
which corporations are formed, is entitled to impose this
charge, not imposed upon natural persons, and other corporations, under like circumstances, as a condition of its
continued future existence, the corporation is not bound
to accept the condition, and go on. No charter can be
forced upon an association of natural persons, and no new
or more onerous conditions can be forced upon a corporation already formed. It may elect to dissolve and retire
from the field of enterprise occupied, rather than accept
the new conditions; and such conditions might be imposed

as would compel that course. *But until accepted they form no part of the charter, and impose no new valid obligations.* An acceptance of the new conditions cannot be presumed while the corporation is protesting that none have been imposed; or, if attempted to be imposed, is insisting that they are invalid, void and of no effect—and in every way, and by all means in its power, is resisting the attempt of the State to give effect to this assumed change in its rights and obligations—while it is still denying the power of the State to make the change and refusing to acquiesce in it. Till the corporation elects to accept the new conditions imposed, or gives some evidence of such election, rather than dissolve, there is no implied promise or obligation to assume the additional burdens laid upon it, or, as in this instance, to pay the additional tax thus imposed *in invitum,* upon which an action can be maintained. This corporation, like every other person, against whom a right is claimed, certainly is entitled to litigate the question, whether any new valid obligations or conditions have been imposed upon it, before it can be called upon to determine whether it will dissolve and retire, or accept the conditions and proceed. *A refusal to accept, surely, can give no right of action, which depends upon acceptance.* If there is any remedy in behalf of the State against a corporation declining to accept, but still continuing to exercise its functions in violation of the existing law, it is by some proceeding in the Courts, in the nature of an information, to dissolve the corporation and wind up its affairs; and this, it appears to me, is the remedy in this case, if there is an amendment to the act under which the defendant is incorporated, imposing the liability of this unequal and unjust tax upon it, as a condition of its continued existence, and the corporation refuses to accept it, or to submit to it.

The doctrine asserted, and sought to be maintained, that because a corporation owes its origin and existence to the State—is a creature of the State—it and all its

belongings are under the arbitrary power and control,
and at the absolute mercy of the State, is monstrous.
The State, through general laws applicable to all similar
corporations, may abolish corporations, may take away
their faculties, may enlarge or restrict their powers and
functions for the future; but it cannot lay its hand upon
their lawful acquisitions or property, otherwise than as
upon the acquisitions and property of natural persons.
Although the title and management of these are vested
in the ideal being called a corporation, the ultimate
property is in the corporators, and their rights in the
property and acquisitions are as sacred in their corporate
as in any other of their relations to society, or to the
State.

Had the State Constitution provided that the property of corporations might be taken for public use
without any compensation, and without a trial or hearing
of any kind, such as for the sites of public buildings, public streets or squares, or for the use of railways, and the
corporations had denied and resisted the validity of such
provision, I apprehend that no Court would hold, that
because it did not immediately dissolve and retire from
business, upon the adoption of such a provision, that it
had been accepted, and thenceforth become one of the
conditions of the future continued existence of the corporation, and in consequence of the fact, that its property
might thenceforth be arbitrarily taken and appropriated
to public use without any hearing or compensation. Yet
such a provision would be no more monstrous than the
doctrine sought to be maintained. Indeed, it is the necessary logical sequence of the doctrine.

From these considerations, and those expressed upon
this point in the *San Mateo Case*, and from the expressed
terms of the Constitution itself, it is clear to me that the
provision in question attempts to provide only for exercising the sovereign power of taxation—has no other end
to accomplish and accomplishes no other purpose; and

that the rights of the parties must be determined on that
hypothesis alone—that is to say, the hypothesis that it
is a tax merely, without any reference to a change of
the fundamental conditions upon which the corporation
is to continue in existence. If not, then that the new
conditions have not been accepted, and there is no ground
upon which this action can be maintained. The suit is
simply one at law for a tax and nothing else, and the
plaintiff must recover on that theory, and on the case
made, or not at all. If this tax can be imposed upon the
defendant, simply because it is a corporation, when it
could not be imposed upon natural persons holding, owning, and using its property under like conditions in all
other respects, then it would be difficult to point out
what rights are left to corporations, or natural persons
in their corporate relations, which the State, under the
Fourteenth Amendment, or otherwise, is bound to respect.

Fifth. At the time of the assessment and levy of the
tax in question there was a deed of trust in existence, and
operative, to secure a large indebtedness, executed by defendant to D. O. Mills and Lloyd Tevis, before the adoption of the present Constitution of the State of California,
which covered the Southern Pacific Railroad, its tracks,
depots, rolling-stock, and all appurtenances—the road
aggregating 1,150 miles in length, of which over 700 are
completed and in operation. It also covered all the lands
granted by the United States to aid in the construction of
said railroad, aggregating, as estimated, 10,000,000 acres,
after excluding reserved lands embraced in the statutory description. This deed of trust, or mortgage, was
duly recorded in the several counties of the State through
which the road extended, and in which the lands were
situated.

A portion of the road, and of the lands mortgaged, was
situated in the county of Santa Clara. The mortgage was
for $46,000 per mile, of which amount bonds have been

issued to the amount of $39,000 per mile. The lands mortgaged, so far as they have been patented, including the lands in Santa Clara County, had been taxed to defendant in the several counties in which they were situated, at their full value, and without any reduction on account of the mortgage, and the taxes duly paid. So, also, no reduction in the amount of the assessed value of the road, rolling-stock, etc., was made in consequence. Thus all the property embraced in the mortgage was taxed to the defendant at its full value, without any reduction in the amount on account of the mortgage. The trust deed contained the following covenant: "And the said party of the first part hereby agrees and covenants to and with the said parties of the second part, and their successors in trust, that it will pay all ordinary and extraordinary taxes, assessments, and other public burdens and charges which may be imposed upon the property herein described and hereby mortgaged, and every part thereof; and the said parties of the second part, the survivor of them or their successors in said trust, or any one or more of the holders of said bonds, may, in case of default of the said party of the first part in this behalf, pay and discharge the same, and any other lien or incumbrance upon said property which may in any way, either in law or equity, be or become in effect a charge or lien thereon, prior to these presents, or to which this mortgage may be subject or subordinate, and for all payments thus made the parties so making the same shall be allowed interest thereon at the rate of seven per centum per annum; and such payments, with the interest thereon, shall be, and are hereby, secured to them by these presents, and declared to be payable and collectable in the same sort of currency or money wherein they shall have been paid, and the same shall be payable by said party of the first part to said parties of the second part upon demand, in trust for the party or parties paying the same, and may be paid out of the proceeds of the sale of said property and franchises hereinbefore provided."

It is gravely and earnestly insisted here that under this covenant the defendant has bound itself to the trustees to pay the whole taxes assessed upon the property covered by the mortgage; that if the tax should be assessed upon defendant and there should be a recovery in this case and payment of the judgment, the defendant would pay no more than it is bound to pay under the covenant in the trust deed, and could not be injured; therefore the tax is valid and a recovery should be had in this action, even though the tax, as levied against the defendant, is unauthorized by any valid law, or was levied without the authority of any law. It would seem to be only necessary to state the proposition to make manifest its fallacy. The proposition in substance is, that if a valid tax had been levied, the defendant had bound itself by a contract to protect a third party, with whom the plaintiff is not in privity against it, by payment or allowing such third party to pay it and make it a secured charge against defendant. And, since this is so, although it is not authorized by any valid law, it would not injure the defendant to levy the tax against it and compel it to pay the whole amount of tax that ought to have been properly levied on somebody on account of the property; therefore the plaintiff ought to recover, although there is no valid tax levied against him or anybody else—no tax for which anybody is now legally liable. Somebody ought to have been made personally liable to pay this tax by a proper and legal assessment of it; and if anybody had been made liable defendant would have been bound to pay it under its covenant, but there was no valid assessment, either against the defendant or anybody else, yet the defendant is personally liable and plaintiff ought to recover. Such is the reasoning presented to us.

This tax, as levied, is either valid, as properly levied under the law, or it is void and its validity must depend upon the law. It cannot depend upon the fact that private parties by an anterior contract, with which the

State and county are not in privity, had a stipulation as to which should pay any tax properly levied. If valid as against defendant so as to make it personally responsible, then the plaintiff is entitled to recover, whether it would be injured or not, and there is no need to invoke the principle that defendant cannot be injured by doing what it is insisted it in good morals ought to do. If the tax as levied is not valid and a legal personal charge upon the defendant under the law, without regard to any contract between private parties as to who shall pay a valid tax upon the land when levied, then there is no valid tax or personal charge against anybody, for no tax purports to have been levied against the trustees in the trust deed, or against the holders of the security. There is no tax upon which the covenant can operate. This action is not based upon moral equities, or even upon equities recognized and enforced by courts of equity. It is a dry action, at law, to recover what is alleged to be a sum of money *legally* due, and for which the defendant is *legally*, personally liable by reason of a valid levy of a tax against it. That is the cause of action alleged, and upon that a recovery must be had, if at all, and according to the *allegata* of the complaint. This is not a suit in equity to enforce a lien for a tax. It is not an application for an injunction against the collection of the tax, in which, possibly, the court might consider whether there were any equities which should call upon it to deny the injunction, or relief, affirmatively sought. It is not a case for the exercise of discretion. It is an action resting upon a strictly legal personal liability. It is not enough that a valid tax to some extent might have been levied. There must be such a tax as throws a legal liability upon the defendant to pay to the plaintiff the sum claimed, or there can be no recovery. But had there been a valid tax levied against the covenantee, or mortgagee, on account of the property, this would not have authorized a recovery against defendant *by reason of the cove-*

nant alone. The covenant cannot affect the case. The covenant was between the defendant and the trustees, for the benefit of the latter, or rather the bond-holders secured, and not for the benefit of the plaintiff. The plaintiff is not in privity with them. But suppose the covenant had been between defendant upon a due consideration, and the trustees, expressly made for the benefit of the plaintiff, in such form, if such could be, as to give plaintiff a right of action on the covenant. It would be necessary to set out the contract on which the right of action rested, and make it the basis or ground of action. Nothing of the kind has been done. The theory of this action is, that a valid tax has been legally assessed against defendant, for which it is personally liable under the Constitution, and a recovery is sought on that ground in the complaint, and upon no other; and it can be had upon no other.

There were two kinds of covenants in use in mortgages and trust-deeds at the time the trust-deed in question was executed; one a covenant that the mortgagor would pay all taxes that might be assessed on the mortgaged property, and in default of payment, that the mortgagee might pay it himself for the protection of his security, and upon such payment that the taxes so paid should be added to the debt, and draw like interest. This was simply to protect his security against other parties who might subsequently acquire liens, and to convert his advances into principal and fix the rate of interest. The purpose of this covenant was not to render the mortgagor liable to pay a tax which he was not already liable to pay, but it was to enable the mortgagee to pay it for his own protection, in case the mortgagor did not, and take away the *voluntary* character of the payment, so that he could convert it into a secured debt, drawing interest as a part of the principal. The other was that the mortgagor would pay not only all taxes levied on the mortgaged property, but also all taxes that should be levied upon the moneys loaned and secured. This was an indirect way of increasing the interest paid on the loan, and imposed an additional burden upon the mortgagor. This last covenant is now forbidden and rendered void under the new Constitution.

The covenant in the mortgage in this case is clearly of the first kind. It only required the mortgagor to pay the taxes or liens *which it was at that time bound to pay without the covenant, and in no way extended its liability.* A law, or constitutional provision, which should compel him to pay the taxes assessed upon the property of the mortgagee, would enlarge his liability beyond that covered by his covenant, and be void. This covenant only extended to taxes for which the defendant was already liable. Besides, if no valid tax has been levied, then the case is not within the covenant, for the defendant cannot be called upon under the covenant to pay a tax absolutely void.

Again, suppose the covenant had been in a mortgage or trust-deed between two natural persons, made at the same time, the sum secured being the whole value of the property. Under the constitutional provision in question, the value of the security, which in the case supposed, is the whole value of the property, must be assessed to the *holder of the security,* and made a personal charge on him alone. It could not be assessed to the *mortgagor,* and made a personal charge or liability on him, and enforced by a suit for a personal judgment; because there is no statute, or constitutional provision, purporting to authorize such a proceeding. Yet he has covenanted with the holder of the security in the same sense as in the trust-deed in question, to pay the whole tax levied on the land, and he would not he injured according to the theory of the plaintiff, if the whole tax should be assessed and recovered against him. If such assessment should be made against the mortgagor instead of the mortgagee without any law for it, or even purporting to authorize it, and a suit be brought to recover a personal judgment for the amount, I

apprehend that no counsel would be found bold enough
to urge that the utter invalidity of the tax is no defence
against the suit, for the reason, that if a proper tax had
been levied against the proper party, he would be bound
by his covenant with *that party* for the protection of that
party's interest, alone to pay the tax, and, therefore, he is
not injured. If such an action under such circumstances
could not be maintained against the mortgagor, then it
cannot be maintained against the mortgagor in this case,
otherwise there is one law for this defendant and another
law for natural persons, occupying in all respects, with reference to their property, precisely the same situation;
and there is a manifest denial of the equal protection of
the laws in this particular, as well as in the others. They
are not equal before the laws. If the constitutional provision in question is void, then there is no law under
which this tax could be levied against defendant, and it is
utterly void and cannot form the basis for a recovery. In
my judgment the provisions of the State Constitution, upon
which the validity of this tax and the right to recover
alone rest, violate the provisions of the Fourteenth Amendment in question, in four vital particulars.

1. They assess railroad and other *quasi* public corporations upon a different basis from that adopted with respect
to natural persons, and other corporations similarly situated with respect to their property in the particulars in
these opinions, and in the opinions in the *San Mateo Case*
pointed out.

2. They provide, with respect to all property other than
railroads operated in more than one county, an opportunity to be heard in the course of the proceeding, to assess
their property before the assessment becomes irrevocably
fixed, while they afford no such notice or opportunity to
be heard with reference to railroads operated in more than
one county, and, in both these particulars, deny to the defendant the equal protection of the laws, within the meaning of the Fourteenth Amendment to the National Constitution.

3. In not affording notice and an opportunity to be heard before the tax becomes finally and irrevocably fixed, they deprive the defendant of its property without due process of law.

4. In assessing a tax and enforcing it as a personal liability against defendant, upon property which it does not own, but which is owned by other parties who pay no tax upon it, the defendant's property, to the extent of the amount taken beyond his proper share of the public burden, is taken for public use, both without due process of law, and without compensation.

As there must be judgment for defendant upon the points arising under the National Constitution, it is unnecessary for us to extend these opinions by examining the questions arising, alone, under the State laws and Constitution, over which we would have had no jurisdiction, but for the fact that the questions already discussed are in the case. Those are questions more properly belonging to the State Courts. We have found the facts in the case, however, and if it should turn out that we are in error upon the points decided, the Supreme Court will be called upon to decide those questions also. If we are not in error, then those questions will, doubtless, be left to the State Courts, where they properly belong.

For the reasons herein, and in the opinion of the presiding Justice stated, in addition to those given in the several opinions delivered in the *San Mateo Case*, I think judgment should be rendered for defendant as directed.

September 17, 1883.

www.ingramcontent.com/pod-product-compliance
Lightning Source LLC
Chambersburg PA
CBHW031439270326
41930CB00007B/787